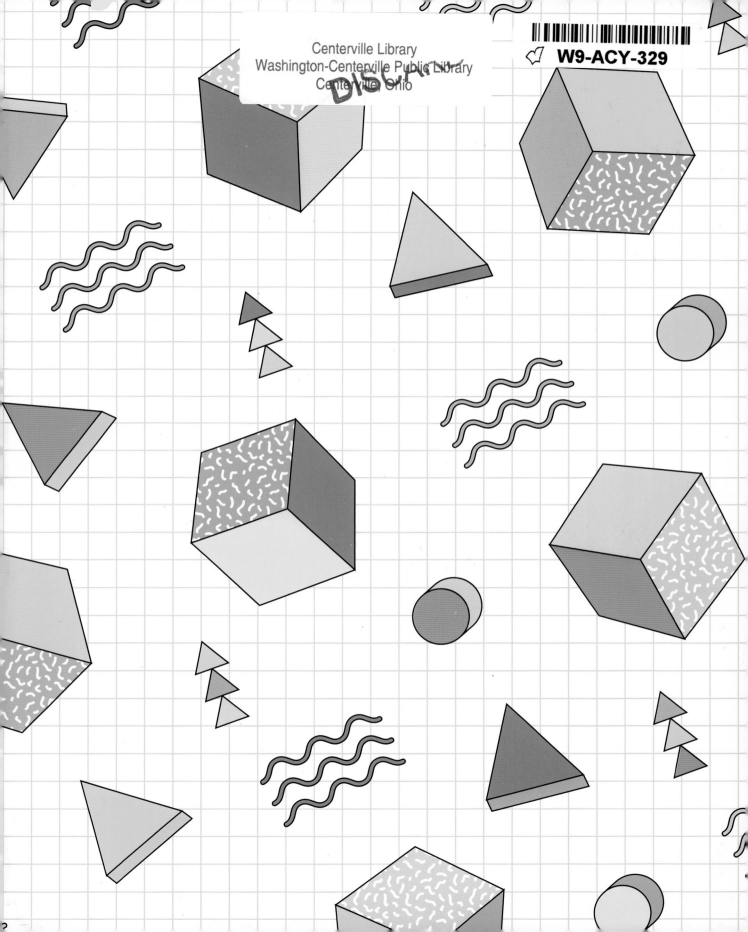

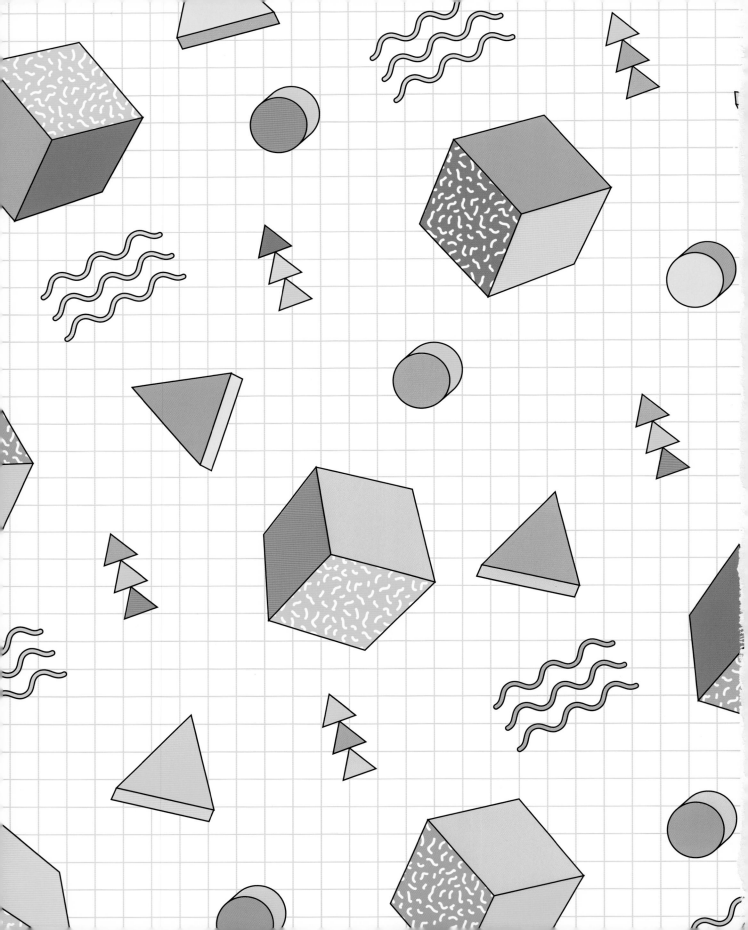

Ranch

Ranch

An Ode to America's Beloved Sauce in 60 Mouth-Watering Recipes

Abby Reisner

DOVETAIL

Copyright © 2018 by Dovetail Press
Text by Abby Reisner
Recipes by Eleanore Park
Photographs by Scott Gordon Bleicher
Art direction, book design, and illlustrations by Chris Santone
Prop styling by Christopher Spaulding

Published by Dovetail Press in Brooklyn, New York, a division of
Assembly Brands LLC.

For details or ordering information, contact the publisher at the
address below or email **info@dovetail.press**.

Dovetail Press
42 West Street #403
Brooklyn, NY 11222
www.dovetail.press

Library of Congress Cataloging-in-Publication data is on file with
the publisher.

ISBN: 978-0-9996612-3-9

First printing, September 2018

Printed in China

10 9 8 7 6 5 4 3 2 1

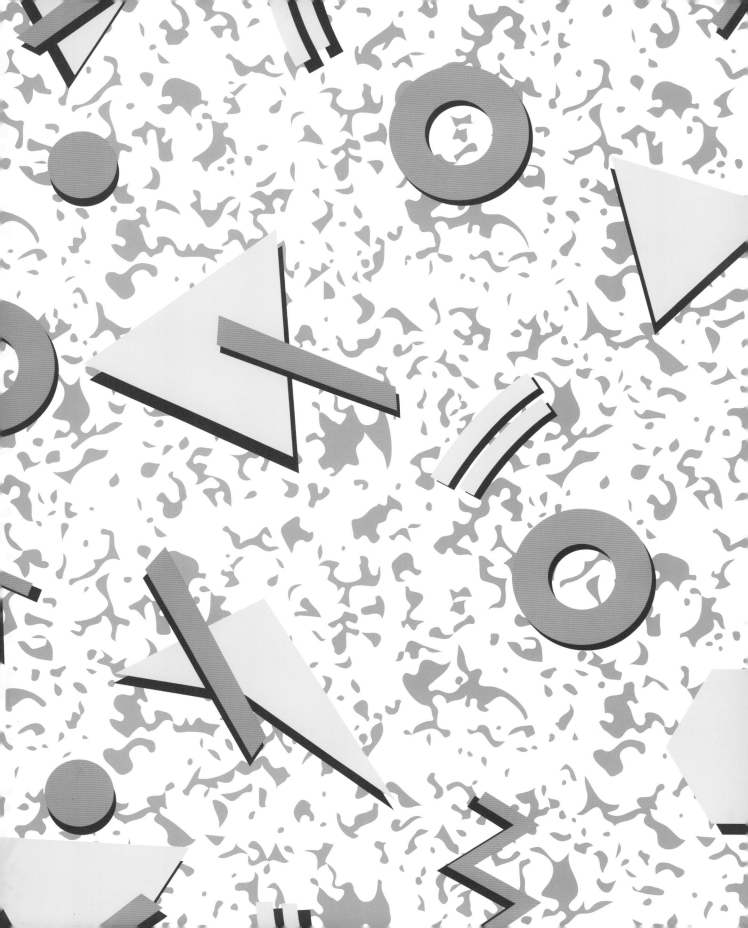

Contents

Introduction

Every Tuesday was pizza night growing up. And while my mom drove to pick up the order, my sisters and I had one job: Prepare the ranch dressing.

Since clearly we were all highly health conscious, pizza was always paired with carrots. We had these shallow blue bowls that were just the right size for fanning out approximately 12 baby carrots around a pool of Hidden Valley Ranch. Then we'd do as my mom did and sprinkle paprika on top in a move that contributed good looks and better taste to the ordeal. Pizza night wasn't complete without this simple addition—and, of course, without ending the meal by swiping the crusts through the ski tracks left by the carrots.

That was my first dance with what some would call a crudités platter, but it taught me that ranch was always to be the heart of it all, both physically and metaphorically. Hummus and guacamole were not yet in my vernacular. Dipping meant ranch. Iceberg lettuce was the only salad green we ate, if you could even call it that. Iceberg lettuce meant ranch.

Spare bottles of ranch dressing were a staple in our house and not just in the obvious places (you know, like the refrigerator). I once discovered my mom's prepper cabinet downstairs, and it held bottles of ranch, tuna fish, and Tupperware. I'm not sure how, but I felt confident that this combination of items would surely save us in the face of a nuclear meltdown.

Fast-forward 20 years, and here I am writing a cookbook all about ranch in order to celebrate this legacy of a condiment. And though I've seen my mom use honey mustard every now and then as I've gotten older, when it comes down to basic survival, I know she'll always choose ranch.

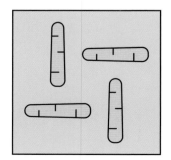 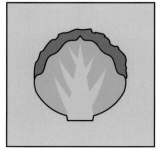 

⟵ Flip book!

American food has a bit of an identity crisis. Take the hamburger, for example. Was it created by a Danish immigrant at a tiny lunch spot in New Haven? Or down in Austin? Or, sorry, it might have actually been the Germans in Hamburg (which definitely sounds like the right answer).

It's soothing then that at least one thing is unequivocally American: ranch dressing. Cool Ranch Doritos are even called Cool American in parts of Europe. At its core, ranch is a simple combination of herbs, dairy, and liquid. Maybe you've seen ranch dressing disguised on menus as "buttermilk" dressing, but ultimately what makes ranch classically ranch is the balance between highbrow and lowbrow. Fresh herbs and dried herbs mingle with mayo to combine into one beautiful package.

~~~~~~~~~

When I mention that I'm writing a cookbook about all things ranch, I invariably get one of two responses. The first is "Oh, like cowboy foods?" As you'll see, the answer isn't exactly no. The second, and more common remark, is saying that their best friend—or their coworker, their sister, their dishwasher repair person—loves ranch. Something lights up in their eyes, as visions of onion powder and dried parsley dance in their heads.

Ranch is not a neutral food. You can hear someone talk about a yellow bell pepper and continue with your day without significant change in blood pressure. But mention ranch dressing and someone within earshot will instantly claim to be its biggest fan, or talk about that crazy time they put ranch on a cinnamon roll by accident only to discover that it was surprisingly good. There will always be one person in the room who feels negative passion, but that's okay: It only encourages advocates to sing its praises louder. I love that I can be at dinner with a group of friends, mention this book, and get some apologetic shrugs from people at the table who'd rather stick their hands in hot lava than be subject to consuming ranch.

Ranch dressing also has a type of Jekyll and Hyde personality. In its earliest iteration, ranch was purely a way to make salad more palatable. But down the road it branched off toward the stretchy pants genre, and we stopped fooling ourselves into thinking that just because ranch could be found on salad, it was healthy.

Ranch's celebrity status and chameleon capabilities merit a place in literary history. In this book, you'll find reasons to fall in love with ranch all over again, revisit classic recipes, and learn how to teach an old condiment new tricks along the way. The recipes are organized in a way that reflects the deep dichotomy of ranch dressing, from old-school

comforts to new-school takes. You'll learn how to make your own dressing, and then tweak it any way you like. But ranch's appeal is in more than its ability to dress up a salad. Ranch-flavored snacks fill the grocery aisles, so not only will you learn how to make your own ranch-dusted snack mix, but you'll also use it to marinate steak and dress up homemade pasta, because even ranch has a tuxedo in the closet. As for dessert? You're on your own.

Ranch isn't just a salad dressing: it's the Great American Condiment. Hot sauce burns you, ketchup activates your acid reflux—but ranch will always soothe. So go ahead and wave your ranch freak flag high, I'll be standing right there next to you.

Ranch Rising

Ranch's cult status begs the question of how a sauce becomes an icon. Food in general has proven many times that it's capable of taking on celebrity status. The Cronut, that halo-shaped love child of a doughnut and a croissant, is a perfect example. And ranch isn't the only sauce that's garnered such a following. Ketchup never quite achieved the cult status of ranch, maybe due to its too-obvious vegetable qualities, but many people swear by it in the same way they do ranch. Then there's sriracha, the chile- and vinegar-based hot sauce that, despite having existed for decades, only recently skyrocketed in popularity.

Somewhere along the way, ranch jumped off the table and into the zeitgeist. When it came into the spotlight as the top-selling dressing in 1992, it landed right into a '90s culture that was big on bold, bright statements, and worshipping trends. People walked around with their Rachel hairstyles wearing jelly shoes and playing with Tamagotchis while listening to Alanis Morissette on their Walkmans. It's unclear who the first genius was to put it on fries or drizzle it over pizza, but it was only a matter of time before it took on a life of its own.

Even chefs at a full range of restaurants around the country are embracing their love for ranch dressing. These are people from the generation who grew up with ranch and are now using it in new and inventive ways. It's also ubiquitous in fast-food chain restaurants, the ultimate landing place for once-niche foods. If you're a buzzy ingredient, landing on a fast-food marquee is the sign that you've made it.

Ranch dressing is more than a Rockwellian relic, and ranch-flavored oddities aren't just stoner food. It's the cement in Americans' hearts (quite literally), and it's not going away any time soon.

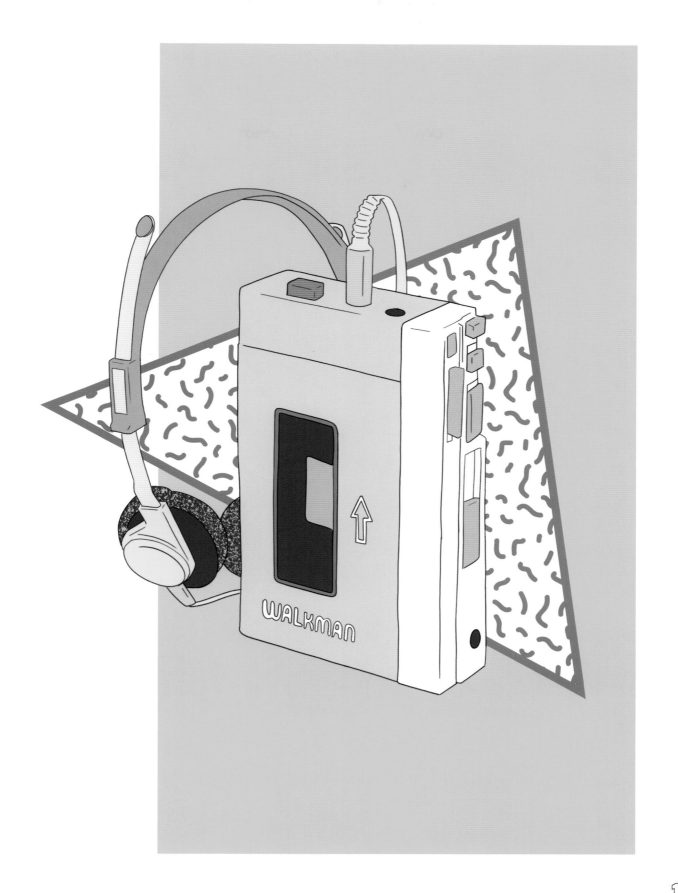

The History of Ranch

1954

A man named Steve Henson opens a ranch outside of Santa Barbara, California, with his wife, Gayle. They name it Hidden Valley Ranch. They are known for their buttermilk-herb dressing and decide to capitalize on people's love for this new delicacy. Operating as a mail-order company, they begin to sell packaged flavorings that are meant to be mixed with buttermilk and mayonnaise, like a boxed cake mix.

1983

Shelf-stable bottled ranch dressing becomes available in grocery stores around the United States—a shockingly recent date.

1972

Clorox senses a gold mine and buys the Hidden Valley Ranch brand for $8 million. It is first advertised as a "party dip," and MSG is unabashedly listed as the second ingredient on the label. Each package costs 39 cents.

1986

Cool Ranch Doritos burst onto the scene in all their blue-bagged glory, marking a departure for ranch from its salad-related uses. They enter the snack bowls and the hearts of humans everywhere, and prove they're here to stay.

2015

An everything-ranch restaurant called Twisted Ranch opens in St. Louis. They serve 31 kinds of ranch dressing, all made in-house. Since that's bound to make decisions impossible, you can get a flight of 13 ranches with your fries.

1992

Ranch pulls ahead of Italian to become the best-selling salad dressing in America.

2017

Hidden Valley releases a whole new level of swag, with bejeweled bottles, ranch fountains, and millennial-geared shirts with the words "Peace, Love, Ranch."

2010

Alinea, a soon-to-be three-star Michelin restaurant in Chicago that's widely known for leading the way in modernist cuisine, has a dish on their menu called "Salad: ranch dressing, soup, powdered." Chef Grant Achatz juxtaposes the foams and pops and bubbles with ranch, proving that no pedestal is too high for ranch dressing to reach.

Ranch Around the World

Ranch itself is highly American, but at its core, it's simply buttermilk and punchy flavorings. Strip this back even further, and it doesn't even have to be buttermilk, just something tangy. The Internet is full of expats or American travelers lamenting a lack of ranch dressing, but other cultures have a long history of using similarly flavored ingredients in their own ways.

~~~~~~~~~~

POLAND: SOS CZOSNKOWY

Sos czosnkowy, which translates to "garlic sauce," is a mayonnaise-based, obviously garlicky condiment that is notoriously excellent on pizza.

FRANCE: TARTAR SAUCE

Think of this like mayonnaise with chopped pickles added. It's often served with seafood.

SPAIN, FRANCE, AND THE MEDITERRANEAN: AIOLI

Just like mayonnaise, aioli is an emulsion of egg and oil, and flavored with garlic.

INDIA: KADHI

Recipes for *kadhi* vary by region, but overall it's a sauce with a buttermilk base that's thickened with chickpea flour and turned a sunny color by various spices. You'll usually find *pakodas*, delightful little fritter dumplings, swimming in it.

MEXICO: JOCOQUE

Jocoque isn't buttermilk, but it's a thick, fermented, sour dairy product that resembles a combo of sour cream and yogurt. It's often used for a type of enchilada called *enjococado*.

Ranch on TV

Ranch Commercials

If the '80s were any indication, everyone was eating salad and everyone was riding horses, sometimes at the same time. At least that's what you'd think after watching a 1986 Hidden Valley TV commercial, which takes about 18 seconds to decipher—is it an episode of *Teletubbies* or a food marketing campaign. But then a mother-daughter duo appears, happily eating their salads in the glow of their bright, shiny futures, and you figure out what's going on.

Flash forward five years to a 1991 commercial, which opens with the sun rising over Hidden Valley Ranch. It's followed by an almost-too-seductive female voice advertising a new shaker bottle product. "All you do is measure, shake, refrigerate, and pour," she says, as if she were looking into the future at a modern-day protein shaker.

In 1994, the company finally caught up to the junk-loving taste buds of their consumers, with a commercial for Pizza Ranch, Taco Ranch, and Nacho Cheese Ranch dressings. As the kids eat their dressing-topped salad, their heads turn into a slice of pizza, cartoon taco, and tortilla chip in turn, which is either the most terrifying thing or the best thing that could ever happen to you.

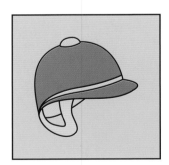 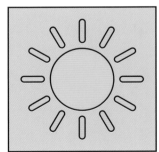 

SNL

Saturday Night Live had its best moments in the '90s. That era brought us classics like "Wayne's World," "Coffee Talk," and pre-*Superstar* Mary Katherine Gallagher. But that was all lead-up to the time-honored 2011 "Taste Test" skit starring Melissa McCarthy as Linda, a no-nonsense

girl who just loves her some ranch. The scene opens on a focus group for three new Hidden Valley Ranch products, where Linda, in all her Spock sweatshirt–wearing, enthusiastic glory immediately starts a solo "HVR" chant. She then goes on to down the ranch samples like they're pudding cups and agonizes her fellow tasters in an attempt to win a cash prize. For her final move, she chugs a bottle of ranch like it's a sports drink and she's just won the championship game. And thus, a challenge was born.

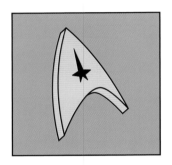  

Eric Andre

One of the recurring bits in comedian Eric Andre's self-titled show involves Andre walking around New York City in a neon crop top with nipple cutouts and a jester hat, bursting into people's personal space with loud, inappropriate, curse-laden declarations of ranch love. This led to a pop-up shop in 2016 selling "Legalize Ranch" T-shirts and dispensing alcoholic ranch dressing, where bottles of ranch sat over ice like they were beers at a party. Much has been said about this definitely-not-PG-rated show, but perhaps this *Village Voice* quote sums it up—and even the essence of ranch dressing itself—best: "It might not make sense, but at least it's uncomplicated."

  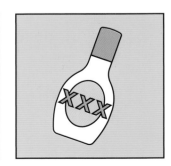

Good Mythical Morning and the YouTube Craze

On one episode of the daily comedy YouTube show Good Mythical Morning, hosts Rhett McLaughlin and Link Neal take everyday food and judge whether or not the "everything is better with ranch" credo applies. They start by drizzling it on a doughnut, making what looks like a Cinnabon-Dunkin' hybrid which they say "doesn't taste like a mistake." They use it in coffee instead of cream, eat ranch-topped crayons (nontoxic, of course) and use it to take uni's classiness down a notch. The sleeper hit proves to be Jello, wiggling under a gloppy heft of ranch—which, when you consider Jello Salad of the '60s, is not all that surprising. Ranch is salad dressing, after all.

This is likely modeled off a BuzzFeed video from a couple years prior that had ordinary people taste test ranch on everything from the innocuous (pizza, mac 'n cheese) to the offensive (Oreos, Nutella). Call it schadenfreude or call it boredom, but there's something irresistible about watching people do terribly gross things that we might not do ourselves. And this is just a sliver of the taste test videos you'll find on the Internet—a dangerous rabbit hole to go down. Don't say I didn't warn you.

 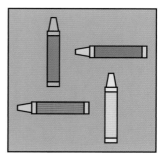 

Choose Your Own Ranchventure

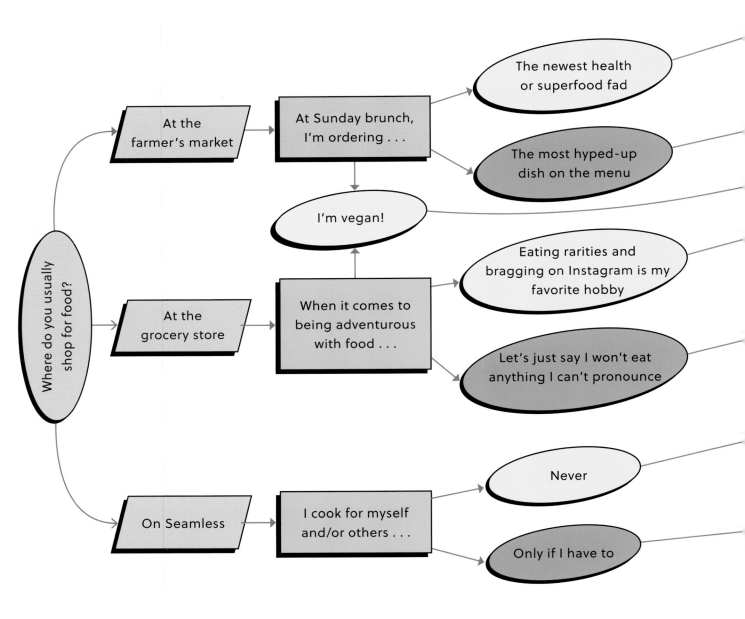

Where do you usually shop for food?

At the farmer's market → At Sunday brunch, I'm ordering . . .
- The newest health or superfood fad
- The most hyped-up dish on the menu
- I'm vegan!

At the grocery store → When it comes to being adventurous with food . . .
- Eating rarities and bragging on Instagram is my favorite hobby
- Let's just say I won't eat anything I can't pronounce

On Seamless → I cook for myself and/or others . . .
- Never
- Only if I have to

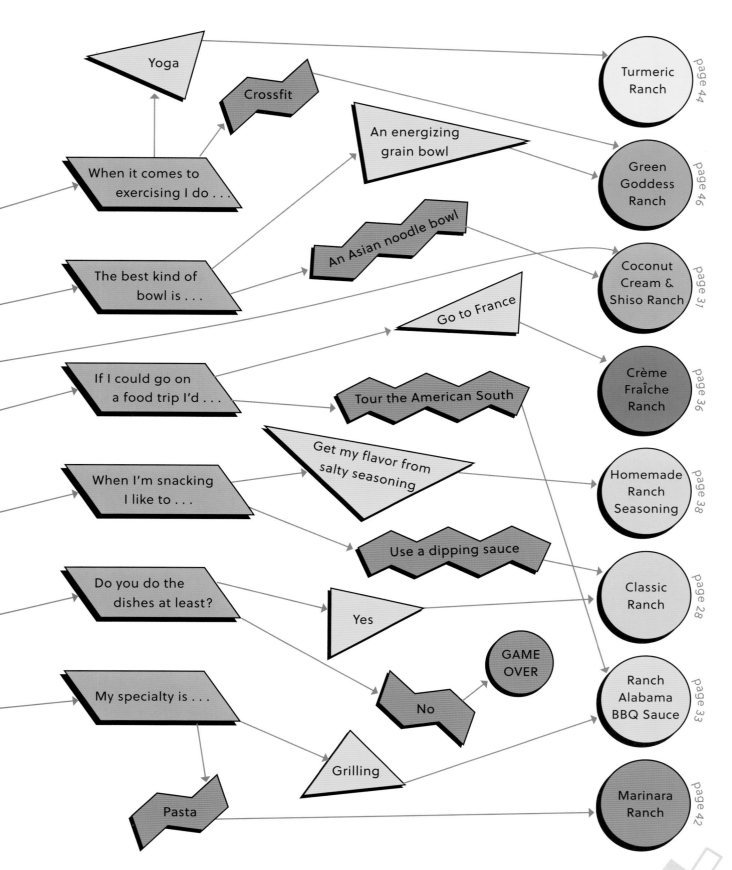

Yoga

Crossfit

When it comes to
exercising I do . . .

An energizing
grain bowl

An Asian noodle bowl

The best kind of
bowl is . . .

Go to France

If I could go on
a food trip I'd . . .

Tour the American South

Get my flavor from
salty seasoning

When I'm snacking
I like to . . .

Use a dipping sauce

Do you do the
dishes at least?

Yes

GAME
OVER

My specialty is . . .

No

Grilling

Pasta

Turmeric
Ranch

Green
Goddess
Ranch

Coconut
Cream &
Shiso Ranch

Crème
Fraîche
Ranch

Homemade
Ranch
Seasoning

Classic
Ranch

Ranch
Alabama
BBQ Sauce

Marinara
Ranch

page 44
page 46
page 31
page 36
page 38
page 28
page 33
page 42

In this chapter you'll find . . .

Pearly Whites

A Rainbow of Ranch

Pearly Whites

This is not just a book about how to make basic ranch dressing at home. If that was all there was to it, I'd stand on the side of the road and hand out a flyer on how to best combine mayonnaise and buttermilk. The core elements of ranch dressing—mayonnaise, dairy, herbs, spices—lend themselves well to variation, making it the blueprint and you the hungry ranch-loving architect.

  Note that many of these require time to sit, in order to let the flavors marry and bloom into the best versions of themselves. I promise it's worth the wait—and it's nothing compared to how long that store-bought bottle sat on the shelf before you used it.

1. Classic Ranch 2. Ricotta Ranch 3. Coconut Cream & Shiso Ranch 4. Labneh & Za'atar Ranch
5. Ranch Alabama BBQ Sauce 6. Greek Yogurt Ranch 7. Crème Fraîche Ranch
8. Sour Cream Ranch 9. Homemade Ranch Seasoning 10. Ranch Compound Butter (sliced)

Classic Ranch

Here it is. The Holy Grail, the North Star, the great white whale. If this recipe was a Web page, it would be called "The One Ranch Dressing Recipe You Need" or "The Ultimate, Foolproof Way to Make Ranch Dressing at Home." The key players are all present—mayonnaise, buttermilk, herbs—but consider it a foundation that lets you build in any direction. Want more herbs? Go for it. Need some heat? Add sriracha or chile oil. The world is your creamy, oniony, high-meets-lowbrow oyster.

Many recipes throughout the book will call for this recipe, in the way you reach out to a best friend for moral support. While you can always substitute store-bought when time (or laziness) necessitates it, I encourage you to go the homemade route when possible. That way, the flavor is up to you from the start, meaning you can add an extra garlic clove or cut back on parsley if that's your style—not to mention the fact that you'll know just how fresh it is.

ingredients

¼ cup sour cream

¼ cup plain Greek yogurt

3 tablespoons mayonnaise

1 teaspoon apple cider vinegar

½ teaspoon Dijon mustard

½ teaspoon onion powder

1 garlic clove, minced

2 tablespoons finely chopped fresh dill

2 tablespoons finely chopped fresh parsley

2 tablespoons finely chopped fresh mint

¼ cup buttermilk

¼ teaspoon Tabasco

Kosher salt

directions

In a medium bowl, combine the sour cream, yogurt, mayonnaise, vinegar, mustard, onion powder, garlic, dill, parsley, and mint. Whisk in the buttermilk, season with Tabasco, and season with salt to taste. Cover and refrigerate for at least 20 minutes or until ready to use. The ranch will keep in an airtight container refrigerated for up to 3 days.

Ricotta Ranch

If there were a baseball team made entirely out of cheese, ricotta would be the utility player: rarely making headlines but can do just about everything. And though fine on its own, it's still batting a thousand when you punch it up with herbs. Add spoonfuls of this ranch to finish a salad or a pasta dish, add it to your eggs or pancakes, or be bold and add it to a baking recipe that calls for ricotta.

ingredients

1½ cups whole milk ricotta cheese

1 tablespoon apple cider vinegar

½ teaspoon mustard powder

½ teaspoon onion powder

2 tablespoons finely chopped fresh dill

2 tablespoons finely chopped fresh parsley

2 tablespoons finely chopped fresh mint

2 tablespoons finely chopped fresh chives

1 tablespoon buttermilk

2 tablespoons Homemade Ranch Seasoning (page 38)

Kosher salt

directions

In a medium bowl, combine the ricotta, vinegar, mustard powder, onion powder, dill, parsley, mint, and chives. Using a rubber spatula, fold in the buttermilk. Add the ranch seasoning and season with salt to taste. Cover and refrigerate for at least 20 minutes or until ready to use. The ranch will keep in an airtight container refrigerated for up to 3 days.

Coconut Cream & Shiso Ranch

Despite all the mayonnaise and buttermilk glory of the classic, ranch can in fact be made vegan with the help of coconut cream (or coconut milk for a more pourable version). Shiso, an herb that has the floral notes of basil and the coolness of mint, is a refreshing addition that balances strong aromas of garlic and onion. Try it as a dressing in a grain bowl or with Buffalo Chicken Wings (page 76) for a decidedly un-vegan pairing.

ingredients

1 small shallot, finely chopped
Juice from 1 lime, plus more to taste
1 cup chilled coconut cream
1 garlic clove, minced
1 teaspoon sumac
2 teaspoons dried minced onion
1 tablespoon finely chopped fresh dill
1 tablespoon finely chopped fresh parsley
2 tablespoons finely chopped shiso leaves
Kosher salt
Freshly ground black pepper

directions

In a medium bowl, combine the shallot and lime juice. Whisk the coconut cream until thoroughly combined (the fat will sometimes separate from the liquid) and add to the bowl. Add the garlic, sumac, minced onion, dill, parsley, and shiso. Season with salt, pepper, and more lime juice to taste. Cover and refrigerate for at least 30 minutes or until ready to use. The ranch will keep in an airtight container refrigerated for up to 3 days.

Labneh & Za'atar Ranch

Labneh, a thick creamy cheese made by straining Greek yogurt and often used in Middle Eastern cuisine, has an inherent tanginess that makes it a natural candidate for ranchification. It begs for the addition of *za'atar*, a spice mixture that's ubiquitous in the same cuisine and features dried herbs, sesame seeds, and salt. Consider this more of a spread than a pourable dressing: Layer it on a sandwich, use it with vegetables in place of hummus, or let it shine as a dipping sauce for Mozzarella Sticks (page 84).

ingredients

2 cups labneh

2 tablespoons buttermilk

1 teaspoon dried mint

1 teaspoon dried parsley

1 teaspoon dried dill

1 teaspoon onion powder

1 garlic clove, minced

Zest and juice from 1 lemon

¼ teaspoon Tabasco

Kosher salt

Freshly ground black pepper

Extra-virgin olive oil, for drizzling

1 teaspoon za'atar

directions

In a large bowl, combine the labneh, buttermilk, mint, parsley, dill, onion powder, garlic, lemon zest, lemon juice, and Tabasco. Mix until smooth and well combined. Season to taste with salt and pepper. Cover and refrigerate for at least 1 hour. The ranch will keep in an airtight container refrigerated for up to 3 days.

When ready to serve, drizzle some oil over the top of the ranch and sprinkle it all over with the za'atar.

Ranch Alabama BBQ Sauce

MAKES ABOUT 2½ CUPS

Alabama white sauce is mayonnaise based, tangy with acid and a peppery bite, and basically a splash of buttermilk short of already being ranch. While so many other BBQ sauces are engineered with meaty brisket or pulled pork in mind, legendary Alabama pitmaster Big Bob Gibson created it in the 1920s specifically for chicken at his eponymous BBQ spot, where they still dunk whole grilled chickens in the stuff. So next time you're diving into a plate of chicken fingers, skip the honey mustard and go with this instead.

ingredients

1½ cups mayonnaise
½ cup sour cream
½ cup apple cider vinegar
1 garlic clove, minced
1 teaspoon finely grated fresh horseradish
¼ teaspoon cayenne
2 teaspoons onion powder
2 teaspoons dried parsley
2 teaspoons dried dill
1 teaspoon sumac
3 tablespoons buttermilk
1 tablespoon Tabasco
1 teaspoon Worcestershire sauce
Kosher salt
Freshly ground black pepper

directions

In a medium bowl, whisk together the mayonnaise, sour cream, vinegar, garlic, horseradish, cayenne, onion powder, parsley, dill, sumac, buttermilk, Tabasco, and Worcestershire. Season to taste with salt and pepper. Cover and refrigerate for at least 1 hour. The ranch will keep in an airtight container refrigerated for up to 1 week.

Greek Yogurt Ranch

Even if you're spice averse, don't fear the Aleppo pepper. The pods are deseeded before they're ground into a powder, meaning it won't burn your face off. Together with sumac, a tangy Middle Eastern spice that's like lemon juice in sprinkle-able form, the two create a version of ranch that lends itself well as a lamb marinade or a way to spruce up Crudités (page 82).

ingredients

¾ cup plain Greek yogurt
1 garlic clove, minced
2 teaspoons onion powder
1 tablespoon sumac
½ teaspoon Aleppo pepper
2 teaspoons white wine vinegar
½ cup buttermilk
1 tablespoon finely chopped fresh dill
1 tablespoon finely chopped fresh parsley
2 tablespoons finely chopped fresh mint
Kosher salt
Freshly ground black pepper

directions

In a medium bowl, combine the yogurt, garlic, onion powder, sumac, Aleppo pepper, and vinegar. Slowly whisk in the buttermilk. Add the dill, parsley, and mint, and whisk to combine. Season to taste with salt and pepper. Cover and refrigerate for at least 30 minutes. The ranch will keep in an airtight container refrigerated for up to 3 days.

Crème Fraîche Ranch

Doing anything the French way instantly says "class," no matter how much you pour onto your plate. With milder crème fraîche in place of sharp yogurt or sour cream, this is a solid gateway dressing, and is basically ranch wearing a beret. It works well in dishes where bold personalities are already in place, like a souped-up Chef's Salad (page 78).

ingredients

1 cup crème fraîche

3 tablespoons mayonnaise

¼ cup buttermilk

3 tablespoons finely chopped fresh basil

3 tablespoons finely chopped fresh parsley

3 tablespoons finely chopped fresh dill

3 tablespoons finely chopped fresh chives

1 garlic clove, minced

1 teaspoon onion powder

1 tablespoon apple cider vinegar, plus
  more to taste

¼ teaspoon mustard powder

3 tablespoons extra-virgin olive oil

Kosher salt

Freshly ground black pepper

directions

In a medium bowl, whisk together the crème fraîche, mayonnaise, buttermilk, basil, parsley, dill, chives, garlic, onion powder, vinegar, and mustard powder. Whisking constantly, slowly drizzle in the oil. Season with salt, pepper, and more vinegar to taste. Cover and refrigerate for at least 30 minutes. The ranch will keep in an airtight container refrigerated for up to 3 days.

Sour Cream Ranch

If you prefer a full-on tang fest where ranch dressing is concerned, skip the mild-mannered mayo and Greek yogurt, and go full speed ahead with just hard-hitting sour cream and a touch of buttermilk to thin it out. It's more condiment than dressing and is best served with Potato Skins (page 88) or as fry sauce.

ingredients

1 cup sour cream
½ teaspoon mustard powder
3 tablespoons finely chopped fresh chives
2 tablespoons finely chopped fresh parsley
2 tablespoons finely chopped fresh dill
1 teaspoon dried minced onion
1 garlic clove, minced
2 tablespoons buttermilk
1 teaspoon apple cider vinegar
Kosher salt
Freshly ground black pepper

directions

In a bowl, combine the sour cream, mustard powder, chives, parsley, dill, onion, and garlic. Slowly add the buttermilk and vinegar, and whisk to combine. Season to taste with salt and pepper. Cover and refrigerate for at least 30 minutes. The ranch will keep in an airtight container refrigerated for up to 1 week.

Homemade Ranch Seasoning

MAKES ABOUT 1 CUP

Problem: Every snack food tastes better when it's made to taste like ranch, but pouring dressing on a bowl of chips creates a soggy mess. Solution: DIY. Ranch. Seasoning. The recipe is easily doubled (or tripled), makes an awesome gift for ranch fanatics, and couldn't be easier to make. Trendy sumac puts the "cool" in cool ranch, but you can omit it without ill effect. You'll learn how to use this homemade seasoning in many ways later in the book—on Ranch-Dusted Popcorn (page 96), in Ranch-Battered Onion Rings (page 108), and even in Homemade Ranch Pasta (page 162). I suggest you make a giant batch to have ready to go, so you can make it rain on anything you'd normally top with the liquid version.

ingredients

6 tablespoons buttermilk powder
1½ tablespoons dried chives
1 tablespoon dried parsley
1 tablespoon dried dill
2 tablespoons onion powder
1 tablespoon garlic powder
1 tablespoon kosher salt
½ teaspoon freshly ground black pepper
¼ teaspoon mustard powder
2 teaspoons sumac (optional)

directions

In a medium bowl, combine the buttermilk powder, chives, parsley, dill, onion powder, garlic powder, salt, pepper, mustard powder, and sumac (if using). Fold the mixture together until well combined. Transfer to an airtight container and store in the refrigerator. The seasoning will keep in the refrigerator for up to 2 months.

Ranch Compound Butter

Ranch Compound Butter solves the issue of cows not producing ranch-flavored milk, meaning we have to take matters into our own hands to get ranch butter. This butter is easy to make and is one of the most versatile recipes in this book—use it for baking Ranch Biscuits (page 110), frying Steak with Watercress and Creamy Horseradish (page 172), or for stuffing Loaded Sweet Potatoes (page 130). Really, the options are endless, and I'm sure you'll come up with your own favorite ways to use it and infuse a subtle ranch flavor into other dishes. This recipe makes the equivalent of two regular sticks of butter, so divide the butter into two sticks before freezing, for easy measuring later.

ingredients

1 cup (2 sticks) unsalted butter, softened

2 tablespoons Homemade Ranch Seasoning (page 38) or store-bought ranch seasoning

directions

In a medium bowl, combine the butter and ranch seasoning. Stir with a rubber spatula until the ingredients are well incorporated. Place half of the butter in the center of a piece of parchment or wax paper in the shape of a log and roll it into a cylinder, then wrap it tightly. Repeat with the other half of the butter.

Transfer the butter to the freezer and freeze completely (it will take about 2 hours). The butter can be made ahead of time and kept for 1 week in the refrigerator or up to 6 months in the freezer.

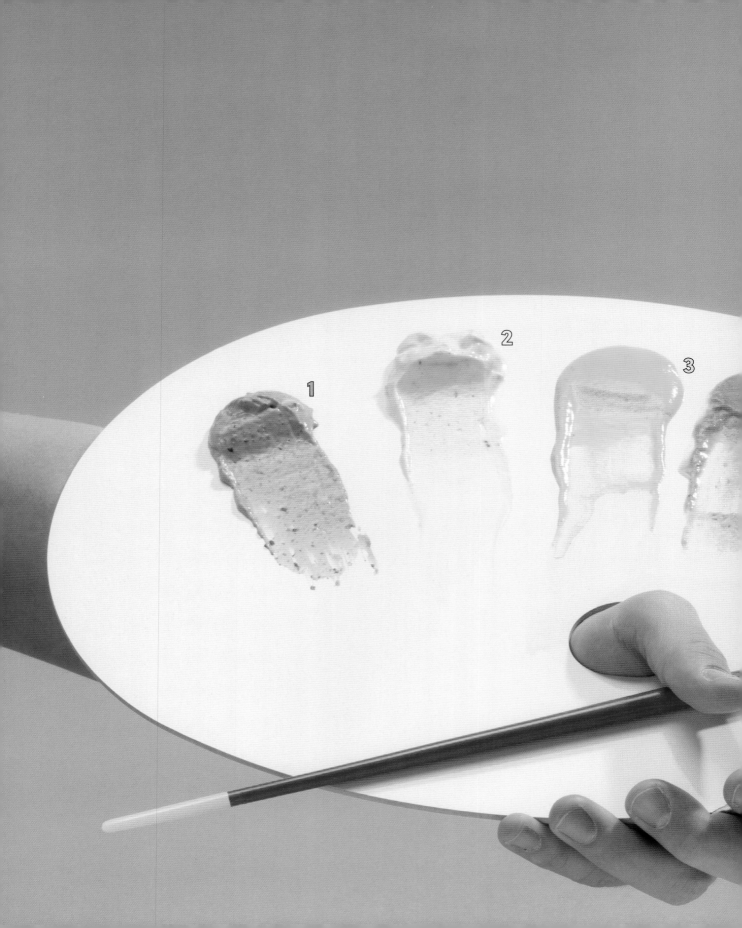

A Rainbow of Ranch

If ranch has one downfall, it's that it's a bit . . . monotonous. That doesn't do it any favors, considering the widely accepted principle that a colorful plate is a healthful one, as though the number of colors in a meal is a yardstick with which to measure our wholesomeness. There's no reason why this Technicolor ideal can't extend to ranch dressing, so follow this color wheel of recipes for a way to add both aesthetic appeal and a spectrum of interesting flavors to the white stuff. Besides, you're better off eating colored ranch dressings than you are a box of crayons.

1. Green Goddess Ranch 2. Turmeric Ranch 3. Roasted Bell Pepper Ranch 4. Marinara Ranch 5. Purple Sweet Potato Ranch

Marinara Ranch

Can't decide if you want to dip your garlic bread in marinara or ranch? Get a sauce that is both. Pair it with pizza or pasta (obviously), or paint the town red by drizzling it over a plate of bell peppers and tomato slices.

ingredients

¼ cup Classic Ranch (page 28) or
   store-bought ranch
1 cup marinara sauce
1 teaspoon Tabasco, or your favorite
   hot sauce
1 teaspoon garlic powder
1 teaspoon onion powder
Kosher salt
Freshly ground black pepper

directions

In a small bowl, combine the ranch, marinara, Tabasco, garlic powder, and onion powder. Season to taste with salt and pepper. Cover and refrigerate for at least 30 minutes. The ranch will keep in an airtight container refrigerated for up to 3 days.

Roasted Bell Pepper Ranch

Roast orange bell peppers for a sweet and tangy ranch, because red peppers shouldn't get to have all the fun. Harissa adds peppery heat here in addition to more orange color. Swirl it into yogurt for a savory snack, or drizzle it on pastas and salads as a vegetable-forward finishing touch.

ingredients

2 large orange bell peppers

5 tablespoons extra-virgin olive oil, plus more for serving

2 cups labneh

¼ cup harissa

1 tablespoon onion powder

2 teaspoons garlic powder

2 teaspoons cayenne

¼ cup buttermilk

Kosher salt

Freshly ground black pepper

directions

Preheat the oven to 450°F. Rub the bell peppers with 1 tablespoon oil and place them on a rimmed baking sheet. Roast the peppers until they begin to deflate and their skin is blistered and blackened all over, about 40 minutes. Transfer them to a medium bowl and cover with plastic wrap. Let the peppers steam for about 20 minutes. Once they are cool enough to handle, peel them and discard the stems and seeds.

In a food processor, combine the roasted pepper flesh, labneh, harissa, onion powder, garlic powder, cayenne, and buttermilk, and season with salt and pepper. Pulse on medium speed until the ingredients are well combined. With the motor running, drizzle in the remaining 4 tablespoons oil and blend until smooth. Transfer the ranch to a bowl and adjust the seasoning if necessary. Cover and refrigerate for at least 30 minutes. The ranch will keep in an airtight container refrigerated for up to 3 days.

Turmeric Ranch

Let us pause for a quick mathematical interlude. If turmeric + milk = golden latte, then turmeric + ranch = golden ranch. The sunny spice has a laundry list of supposed health benefits (anti-inflammatory, antioxidant, whatever "detoxifying" means), but deserves just as much attention for its earthy taste, which balances the bright Greek yogurt. Use it in the Quinoa Grain Bowl (page 158) to achieve health nirvana.

ingredients

1 tablespoon turmeric
½ cup Greek Yogurt Ranch (page 34)
1 tablespoon nutritional yeast
1 tablespoon fresh lemon juice
3 tablespoons extra-virgin olive oil
Kosher salt

directions

In a small bowl, combine the turmeric, ranch, nutritional yeast, and lemon juice. Whisking constantly, slowly drizzle in the oil. Season to taste with salt. Cover and refrigerate for at least 30 minutes. The ranch will keep in an airtight container refrigerated for up to 3 days.

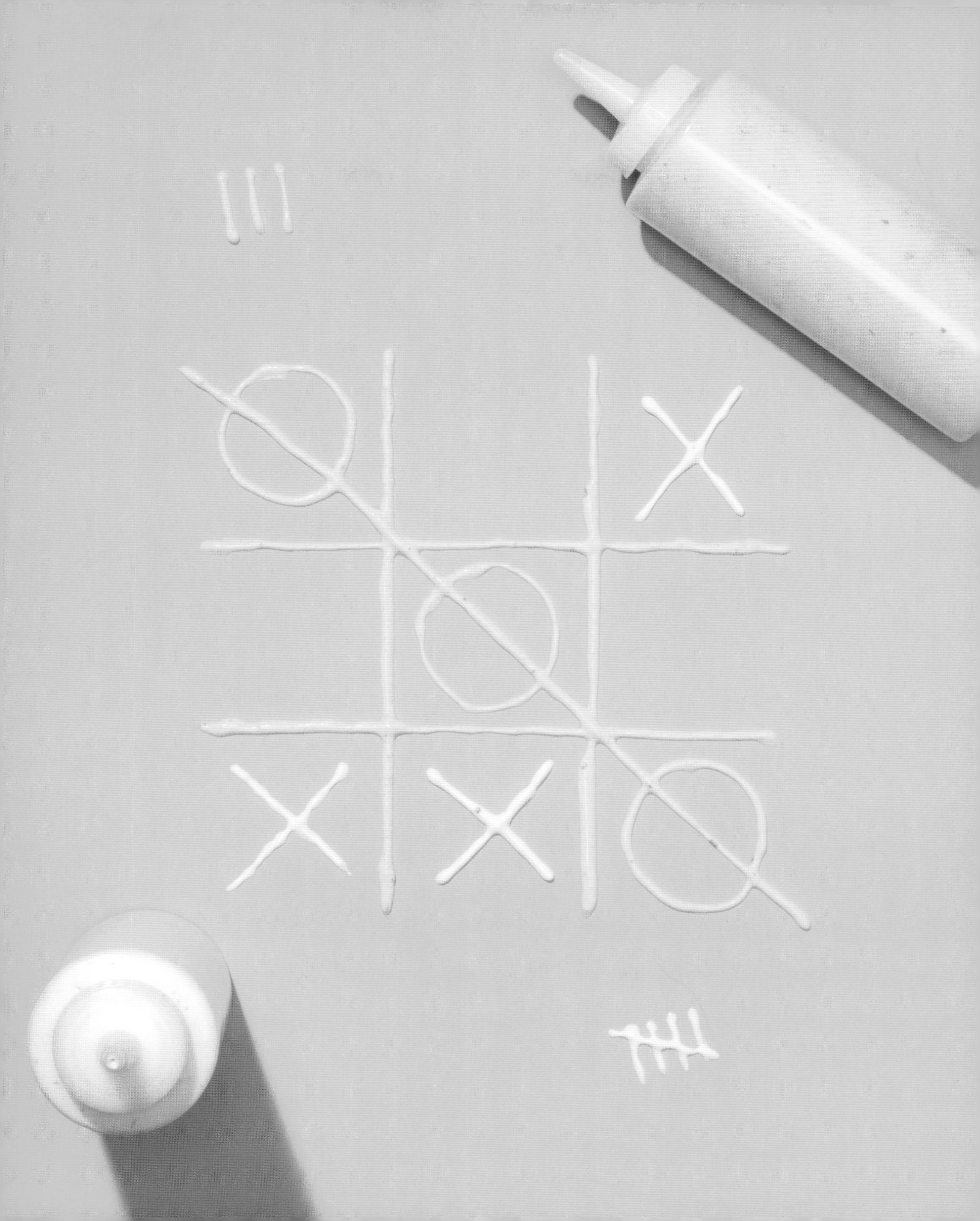

Green Goddess Ranch

Ranch and green goddess dressing lead parallel lives. They're both creamy, herb-laden snack vehicles cutely disguised as "salad dressing," that seem destined to be combined. Use it like a dip with fittingly green items like sliced cucumber, celery, and summer squash, or stay true to its dressing roots by pouring it over the Mixed Lettuce Salad peppered with pepita seeds and sliced fennel (page 134).

ingredients

1 small shallot, finely minced
1 tablespoon fresh lemon juice
1 teaspoon white wine vinegar
¼ cup mayonnaise
¼ cup sour cream
½ ripe Hass avocado
¼ teaspoon onion powder
¼ cup loosely packed fresh tarragon leaves
¼ cup loosely packed fresh parsley leaves
⅛ cup loosely packed fresh chervil leaves
⅓ cup loosely packed fresh basil leaves
2 anchovy fillets, roughly chopped
1 small garlic clove
Kosher salt
Freshly ground black pepper
¼ cup extra-virgin olive oil

directions

In a bowl, combine the shallot, lemon juice, and vinegar. Let sit for 10 minutes.

In a blender or a food processor, combine the shallot mixture, mayonnaise, sour cream, avocado, onion powder, tarragon, parsley, chervil, basil, anchovies, and garlic; season with salt and pepper. Blend on medium speed while slowly drizzling in the oil. Scrape down the sides and adjust seasoning if necessary. Continue blending until the dressing is smooth and only showing a few specks of the herbs. If it seems too thick, add a tablespoon of water and pulse a few more times to incorporate. The ranch will keep in an airtight container refrigerated for up to 3 days.

Purple Sweet Potato Ranch

Remember the purple ketchup craze? Kids of the '90s got a Technicolor delight with the Heinz product that burst onto the scene at the turn of the millennium. Ranch hasn't forgotten about this phase either, and it feels left out. In this recipe, you'll combine purple sweet potatoes with ranch flavors, because "nobody puts Baby in the corner." Serve this colorful delight with some toasted slices of sourdough bread.

ingredients

2 medium purple sweet potatoes

½ cup tahini

2 garlic cloves, minced

2 tablespoons labneh

1 tablespoon onion powder

Juice from ½ lemon, plus more to taste

Kosher salt

Freshly ground black pepper

¼ cup extra-virgin olive oil

2 tablespoons chopped fresh dill

Flaky sea salt, for serving

directions

Preheat the oven to 450°F. Line a rimmed baking sheet with aluminum foil. Pierce the potatoes all over with a fork and transfer to the prepared baking sheet. Roast the potatoes until fork-tender, about 25 minutes, and let cool.

Once the sweet potatoes are cool enough to handle, peel off the skin. In a food processor, combine the potatoes, tahini, garlic, labneh, onion powder, and lemon juice. Season with salt and pepper. Pulse until the ingredients are well combined. With the motor running, drizzle in the oil and blend until smooth. Transfer the ranch to a medium bowl. Mix in the dill and adjust the flavor with more salt, pepper, and lemon juice. Cover and refrigerate for at least 20 minutes. The ranch will keep in an airtight container refrigerated for up to 3 days.

When ready to serve, top the ranch with flaky sea salt.

Pop Art:
Ranch Soda

There are some things you do because you want to do them. There are other things you do because you have to do them. Then there are things you do because someone's asked you to do them. Drinking a bottle of ranch-flavored soda falls into none of these categories, but here I am, a bit fizzier and corn syrupy than I was before.

Rocket Fizz is a nostalgic candy and soda shop with franchised locations around the country, and they have a line of food-flavored sodas, as if it were some twisted precursor to the juicing trend. The best-selling of the bunch is bacon, with other options including peanut butter and jelly, buffalo wing, and of course, ranch dressing. There's no crazy backstory behind it. No lucid dreams or bold dares. Just Rob Powells and Ryan Morgan, the company's founders, poking fun in beverage form at how much ranch dressing Morgan uses.

This seemed like a necessary part of research, so I ordered a few bottles to try myself. The first step was to evaluate the smell, which was somewhere between essence of dirty toe Band-Aid and that time the family goldfish died but no one realized it for five days. Hence, I expected the absolute worst. I sat at my desk with a line-up of water, seltzer, a glass of wine, and a bowl of carrots for reinforcement, as if this combination of items could outweigh any bad taste that I was about to experience. Maybe it was my strict adherence to "hope for the best, prepare for the worst," but it honestly was not the weirdest thing I've ever tasted. It just tasted like sugar water! With the aftertaste of onion ring! It definitely didn't taste *good*, but after that smell, anything short of live ferret would have been a relief.

This drink was not intended to replace a daily ginger ale habit, but I didn't stop at one sip, so take that as you will.

In this chapter, you'll find . . .

Take a Dip

For my six-year-old niece, every meal is a new opportunity for dipping. Each piece of lettuce gets individually dipped in the dressing, ketchup puddles are a necessity no matter the dish, and pancakes don't pass Go without collecting maple syrup. This all goes to say that from an early age, we're well versed in the culinary tenet that delicious dipped in delicious equals delicious.

Ranch lends itself well to various dips and spreads, as it's already a monarch of the crudités platter and is naturally thicker than other dressing counterparts. Dips—especially ranch—go just as well with cut vegetables as they do with potato chips, making this a good way to straddle the health food/comfort food split personality of ranch dressing. But don't stop at just classic ranch. Combine the best of all dip worlds by letting ranch join forces with the likes of hummus, guacamole, and caramelized onions, in order to make an end product that's greater than the sum of its parts.

Herbed Feta Ranch Dip

This is the Greek answer to Ricotta Ranch, a pepper-less version of the staple meze *tirokafteri*. Just like in the famous Greek cheese dip, the tanginess comes from feta and everything is blended to silky perfection. Top it with a heavy dose of fresh herbs to counter all the salty cheese, then dig into it with some cucumber, radish, celery, or carrot sticks. Or just a spoon.

ingredients

1¾ cups feta (about 9 ounces), crumbled

¼ cup buttermilk

3 tablespoons chopped fresh parsley, plus torn leaves for garnish

3 tablespoons chopped fresh chives, plus more for garnish

3 tablespoons chopped fresh dill, plus torn sprigs for garnish

2 tablespoons chopped fresh basil, plus torn leaves for garnish

1 teaspoon sumac (optional)

1 teaspoon onion powder

Juice from ½ lemon

Kosher salt

Freshly ground black pepper

¼ cup extra-virgin olive oil

directions

In the bowl of a stand mixer fitted with a paddle attachment, combine the feta, buttermilk, parsley, chives, dill, basil, sumac (if using), onion powder, and lemon juice. Season with salt and pepper. Beat on medium-low to combine ingredients. Continue to beat the mixture and slowly drizzle in the oil in a steady stream until well incorporated. Cover and refrigerate for at least 30 minutes. The dip will keep in an airtight container refrigerated for up to 3 days.

When ready to serve, transfer the dip to a medium bowl and top with parsley, chives, dill, and basil.

Caramelized Onion Ranch Dip

Onion dip and ranch dressing both know what it's like to be ostracized. While everyone was busy turning up their noses at these flavor-bomb packets, they stuck to their shelf-stable roots and outlived the haters. This recipe seeks inspiration from that old pantry hero, but calls on fresh ingredients and heady caramelized onions. For a thicker version, substitute the whole milk yogurt with Greek yogurt. Pair with potato chips for a snack that'll throw you back to the first "fancy" cocktail party you ever went to.

ingredients

3 tablespoons unsalted butter
¼ cup vegetable oil
2 medium yellow onions, thinly sliced
¼ teaspoon cayenne
Kosher salt
Freshly ground black pepper
1 cup whole milk yogurt
½ cup mayonnaise
½ cup sour cream
2 garlic cloves, minced
2 scallions, green parts only, finely
    chopped
2 tablespoons chopped fresh dill
2 tablespoons chopped fresh parsley
3 tablespoons chopped fresh chives
2 teaspoons buttermilk

directions

In a large skillet, melt the butter and heat it with the oil over medium heat. Add the onions and cayenne, and season with salt and pepper. Cook, stirring often, until the onions are soft and golden, about 10 minutes. Reduce the heat to low and continue to cook, stirring occasionally, until the onions are deeply brown and caramelized, about 20 minutes. If the onions begin to stick to the skillet, add a tablespoon of water and stir, scraping the bottom of the skillet. Remove the skillet from the heat and allow to cool completely.

In the bowl of a stand mixer fitted with a paddle attachment, combine the caramelized onions, yogurt, mayonnaise, sour cream, garlic, scallion greens, dill, parsley, chives, and buttermilk. Beat on medium-low until the ingredients are well combined and the texture is smooth. Season to taste with more salt and pepper. The dip will keep in an airtight container refrigerated for up to 3 days.

Ranch Baba Ghanouj

MAKES 1¾ CUPS

Baba ghanouj benefits from lots of fresh herbs as a balance to the eggplant's earthiness. I challenge you to cook the eggplants as long as you can and not freak out about burning them. Go until they seem nearly deflated from being under the broiler, as the further you take it, the more flavorful your final product will be. Serve this ranchy baba ghanouj as an appetizer or a side dish, alongside the usual suspects: pita, crudités, or toasted crusty bread.

ingredients

4 medium Italian eggplants (about 2½ pounds)
2 garlic cloves, minced
3 tablespoons tahini
¼ cup labneh
Juice from 1 lemon, plus more to taste
2 teaspoons onion powder
¼ cup chopped fresh parsley, plus torn leaves for garnish
2 tablespoons chopped fresh dill, plus sprigs for garnish
2 tablespoons chopped fresh mint, plus torn leaves for garnish
1 scallion, finely chopped
¼ cup extra-virgin olive oil, plus more for drizzling
Kosher salt

directions

Prepare a broiler for high heat and arrange the oven rack in the upper third of the oven. Line a rimmed baking sheet with aluminum foil.

Place the eggplants on the baking sheet and bake directly under the broiler, turning halfway through, until the eggplants are charred all over and tender, about 45 to 60 minutes. Remove from the oven and carefully wrap and seal the eggplants with aluminum foil to create a package (this will steam the eggplants allowing for their skins to peel off easily). Set aside for 15 minutes.

Once the eggplants are cool enough to handle, unwrap them, scoop out the flesh, and transfer it to a strainer. Press gently on the eggplants to let out any excess moisture. Discard the skins.

In a large bowl, combine the eggplants, garlic, tahini, labneh, lemon juice, onion powder, parsley, dill, mint, and scallion. Using a fork, mash the ingredients together until well combined. Add the oil in a steady stream, mixing the ingredients constantly with a fork. Season with salt and more lemon juice to taste. Drizzle more oil all over. The dip will keep in an airtight container refrigerated for up to 2 days.

When ready to serve, transfer the dip to a medium bowl and top with parsley, dill, and mint.

Ranch Hummus

Adding ranch to this popular dip builds on the creaminess that tahini supplies, giving it a cloudlike fluffiness that you wouldn't typically associate with ranch dressing. I'm not going to pretend I'm the type to always have homemade dressings in my refrigerator, and I won't assume you are, either. So go ahead and use store-bought ranch dressing here—it's only a couple of tablespoons, after all. If you are going full effort though, keep with the Mediterranean theme by using Labneh & Za'atar Ranch (page 32) or Greek Yogurt Ranch (page 34) as your ranch of choice. I don't need to tell you the many ways you can use hummus, but if you need a starting point, this utilitarian dip is a pita chip's best friend.

ingredients

1 (15-ounce) can chickpeas, rinsed and
   drained
½ cup tahini
3 tablespoons fresh lemon juice
1 garlic clove, minced
2 tablespoons store-bought ranch dressing
1 tablespoon chopped fresh dill, plus more
   for garnish
1 tablespoon chopped fresh parsley, plus
   more for garnish
Kosher salt
Freshly ground black pepper
¼ cup extra-virgin olive oil, plus more for
   drizzling

directions

In a food processor, combine the chickpeas, tahini, lemon juice, garlic, ranch, dill, parsley, and 2 tablespoons water. Season with salt and pepper. Pulse on medium speed until the ingredients are well combined and smooth. With the motor running, slowly add the oil in a steady stream. Continue to process until hummus is very smooth and creamy. Adjust the seasoning if necessary. The hummus will keep in an airtight container refrigerated for up to 3 days.

When ready to serve, transfer the hummus to a small bowl. Drizzle with more oil and top with dill and parsley.

Ranch Guacamole

The New York Times caused an uproar in 2015 when they suggested adding peas to guacamole, in what many saw as an unnecessary, nonsensical bastardization of a traditional Mexican dish. Maybe so, but they weren't trying to stay within the four walls of the guac box—and neither is Ranch Guacamole. It makes the already velvety dip impossibly smooth, turning it into a hybrid sandwich spread/chip accompaniment. Serve it with Ranch-Flavored Tortilla Chips (page 100) if you're truly devoted.

ingredients

¾ cup sour cream
¼ cup buttermilk
1 teaspoon onion powder
1 teaspoon dried parsley
4 large ripe Hass avocados, halved
Juice from 1 lime, plus more to taste
½ jalapeño, cored, seeded, and finely chopped
¼ white onion, finely chopped
Kosher salt
Freshly ground black pepper
3 tablespoons chopped fresh cilantro, plus more for garnish
3 tablespoons chopped fresh chives
Toasted pepitas, for garnish (optional)

directions

In a large bowl, whisk together the sour cream, buttermilk, onion powder, and parsley. Add the avocados, lime juice, jalapeño, and onion. Season with salt and pepper to taste. Mash the ingredients together with a fork until well combined. Stir in the cilantro and chives. Add more salt or lime juice to taste.

Transfer the guacamole to a bowl and top with toasted pepitas (if using) and more cilantro. Serve immediately.

Pimento Cheese Ranch Dip

Pimento cheese is used to having its limbs pulled in different directions. The so-called "caviar of the South" is used in grilled cheese, served with fries, spread onto grits, and has been equated to the "peanut butter of Southern childhoods." With the mayonnaise and dairy already built in, it's one seasoning packet away from becoming a variation on ranch. Calabrian chiles add heat and funk if you choose to include them, but they can be easily omitted for a tamer version. Serve this dip with Ritz crackers or other similar crunchy snack foods.

ingredients

2 cups freshly grated sharp cheddar cheese

1 cup mayonnaise

4 ounces cream cheese, softened

¼ cup pimiento peppers from a jar, drained and diced, or roasted red peppers, finely chopped

½ teaspoon cayenne

1 teaspoon onion powder

1 teaspoon dried dill

1 teaspoon dried parsley

2 Calabrian chile peppers, finely chopped (optional)

Kosher salt

Freshly ground black pepper

2 tablespoons chopped fresh chives, for garnish

directions

In the bowl of a stand mixer fitted with a paddle attachment, combine the cheddar cheese, mayonnaise, cream cheese, pimiento peppers, cayenne, onion powder, dill, parsley, and Calabrian chiles (if using), and blend on medium speed. Season with salt and pepper to taste, and continue to blend until the ingredients are well combined. The dip will keep in an airtight container refrigerated for up to 3 days.

When ready to serve, transfer the dip to a bowl and top with the chives.

Smoked Trout Ranch Dip

Before you question this pairing, consider how standard-issue smoked trout dip and ranch dressing share the same mayonnaise and sour cream foundation. Smoked fish is already often served with chives, onion, and dill, so it's only natural to throw everything in the ranch pool and take a dip. As for flotation devices? Go with crackers, bagels, or toast.

ingredients

1 large shallot, finely chopped

Juice from ½ lemon

8 ounces smoked trout, skin and bones removed, flaked

½ cup mayonnaise

½ cup sour cream

½ teaspoon onion powder

½ teaspoon dried parsley

½ tablespoon prepared horseradish, like Gold's

2 tablespoons chopped fresh chives, plus more for garnish

2 tablespoons chopped fresh dill, plus sprigs for garnish

Kosher salt

Freshly ground black pepper

directions

In a bowl, combine the shallot and lemon juice. Allow the shallot to soften in the lemon juice for at least 10 minutes. Add the trout, mayonnaise, sour cream, onion powder, parsley, horseradish, chives, and dill, and stir to combine. Season to taste with salt and pepper. The dip will keep in an airtight container refrigerated for up to 3 days.

When ready to serve, transfer the dip to a bowl and top with more chives and some dill sprigs.

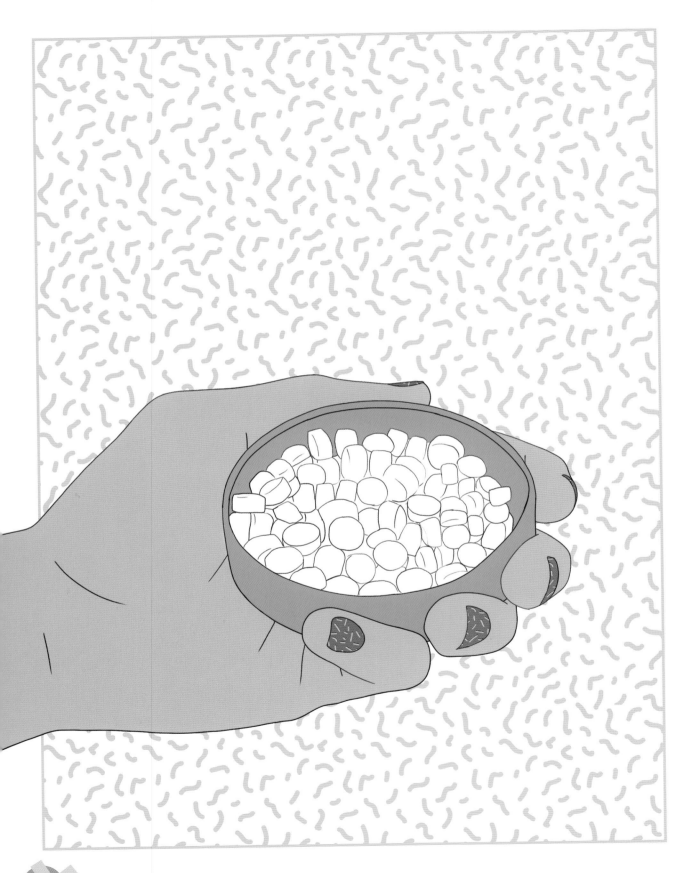

Fresh Take:
Ranch Flavored Mints

I have a good friend who once told me a story about how her sister would eat ranch dressing and then chase her around the house with "ranch breath." Sometimes she would eat ranch on purpose just as a ploy for revenge, because that's what sisters are for. It's a move that could traumatize anyone—a heavy-breathing dragon of a sister exhaling buttermilk and onion—a scene that still haunts my friend 20 years later.

This cat-and-mouse game could have been made even more terrifying for my friend by a product that popped up a few years ago: Ranch Flavored Mints. They come in an adorable tin that belies the nature of the beast within, an innocent "candy" that tastes as though someone tried to repackage ranch dressing into solid food that an astronaut could take into space.

You can watch plenty of videos online of people trying these out, most of whom are in that sweet spot of newfound Internet freedom called middle school. It's as if one year, everyone got these in their Christmas stocking and felt the need to broadcast them to the world. To me, Ranch Flavored Mints fall into the same category as Chia Pets or Pogs—novelty gifts that don't make any sense in the context of the world, but are always exciting and will inevitably end up in the hands and mouths of children.

In this chapter, you'll find . . .

Classics with a Twist

We've all been 10 years old. We all know how exciting pizza is, and that mozzarella sticks are as close to heaven as we'll get in this world. But then the novelty wears off, and honey mustard or mortal ketchup just doesn't do it for chicken tenders anymore, and then what are we to do? Eat greasy, soul-affirming food without a sauce lathered all over it? Thank you for saving us from that, ranch dressing.

Rather than just bringing back the usually frozen-and-defrosted snacks you ate after school every day—or in a diner before stumbling home at 2 a.m. last Saturday night—each of these classics has a way to turn it up to 11, by swapping out standard ranch for a more modern version. If we can have wine pairings, we can certainly tailor our ranch dressings to the grease bombs they fit with best.

Buffalo Chicken Wings

with Coconut Cream & Shiso Ranch

For whatever reason, "chicken wings" and "sporting events" are like the peanut butter and jelly pairing of the bar snack world. This messy but delicious affair was invented in the '60s at a small family restaurant in Buffalo, where it was always paired with blue cheese, but swapping in a (vegan!) coconut cream ranch makes eating chicken wings feel practically virtuous. Refreshing shiso helps tame the beast that is Frank's RedHot, and entry-level hot sauce users can scale back by starting with one-third cup and adding more as needed.

ingredients

Kosher salt

Freshly ground black pepper

2 teaspoons ground cumin

2 teaspoons paprika

4 teaspoons cornstarch

3 pounds chicken wings—wing tips removed, separated at the joint, patted dry

⅔ cup Frank's RedHot, or other hot sauce

3 tablespoons unsalted butter

Canola oil, for frying

Coconut Cream & Shiso Ranch (page 31), for serving

Celery and carrot sticks, for serving

directions

In a large bowl, combine a generous amount of salt and pepper with the cumin, paprika, and cornstarch. Add the chicken wings and toss to coat evenly. Place a cooling rack over a rimmed baking sheet. Shaking off excess dry mixture, transfer the seasoned chicken wings to the cooling rack and refrigerate, uncovered, overnight.

Remove the chicken wings from the refrigerator and allow them to warm to room temperature, about 30 minutes. Meanwhile, in a small saucepan over low to medium heat, combine the hot sauce and butter. Stir until the butter is melted and the sauce comes together, about 5 minutes. Season with salt and pepper to taste. Remove the sauce from heat and set aside.

Line another rimmed baking sheet with 3 layers of paper towels and set a clean cooling rack over it. In a large saucepan, heat 3 inches of oil over medium heat until an instant-read thermometer reads 350°F. Working in batches (don't overcrowd the pan), fry the chicken wings until golden brown and crispy on all sides, about 12 to 15 minutes, turning occasionally. Using a slotted spoon or tongs, transfer the chicken wings to the cooling rack. Season the chicken wings with more salt while still warm (if the chicken wings start getting cold, gently rewarm them all the way through in a 300°F oven).

Transfer the warm chicken wings to a large bowl and toss with the sauce (if the sauce is cold, rewarm it on the stove before tossing).

Serve the chicken wings with the ranch and celery and carrot sticks.

Chef's Salad

with Crème Fraîche Ranch

Just as there are mother sauces in French cuisine, certain dishes form the core of America's salad inventory—Cobb, Waldorf, Caesar—and the often-overlooked chef's salad is certainly one of them. Is it a cold-cut sandwich role-playing as salad? Definitely. Does that make it any less worthy? Definitely not. The non-negotiables are all here, like hard-boiled eggs and matchstick-shaped cheese, but they're joined by a mild crème fraîche ranch dressing that brings everything together without stealing the spotlight.

ingredients

2 large eggs

8 cups mixed torn lettuces, such as Boston, Bibb, red leaf, and chopped romaine hearts

1½ cups shredded rotisserie chicken breast

3 ounces cured American ham slices

1 cup Sungold or cherry tomatoes, halved

1 ripe Hass avocado, diced

1 (3-ounce) block Swiss cheese, cut into matchsticks

1 (3-ounce) block sharp yellow cheddar cheese, cut into matchsticks

2 Persian cucumbers, cut into ½-inch slices

Kosher salt

Freshly ground black pepper

Créme Fraîche Ranch (page 36)

directions

Fill a large bowl with ice and cold water and set aside. In a medium saucepan, bring water to a boil, add the eggs, and cook for 8 minutes. Using a slotted spoon, remove the eggs and immediately transfer them to the ice bath. Let the eggs cool completely and remove them from the ice bath. Peel them and cut them into halves, then set aside.

Place the mixed lettuces on a large plate. Arrange the chicken, ham, tomatoes, avocado, Swiss, cheddar, cucumbers, and the eggs over the lettuces so that each ingredient is separated into its own individual section. Season with salt and pepper.

Drizzle spoonfuls of the ranch all over the salad, and serve immediately with extra ranch on the side.

Chicken Tenders

with Ranch Alabama BBQ Sauce

I consider myself a chicken tender expert. The first recipe I ever cooked was Cereal-Crusted Chicken Tenders from a Beanie Babies cookbook when I was 10 years old. Growing up, dinner at Burger King with my mom was a regular occurrence. And we always had chicken, never burgers. From this health conscious time of my life, I have one single regret—I never dipped my chicken tenders in anything. Just dry pieces of breaded white meat, straight to the face, without even a french fry chaser. If I could do that phase of my life over again, I would make sure every chicken tender made its way into ranch-spiked Alabama white BBQ sauce. It's probably what the cool kids were all doing—but I wouldn't know. I was too busy parading around in a paper Burger King crown.

ingredients

1½ pounds boneless, skinless chicken
   breasts, cut lengthwise into 1¼-inch strips
Kosher salt
Freshly ground black pepper
2 tablespoons mayonnaise
1 tablespoon sour cream
1 teaspoon Dijon mustard
2 teaspoons smoked paprika
1 large egg
½ cup canola oil
2 cups panko breadcrumbs
Ranch Alabama BBQ Sauce (page 33),
   for serving

directions

Preheat the oven to 450°F with a rack positioned in the middle. Place a cooling rack over a rimmed baking sheet. Pat the chicken strips dry with paper towels. Season liberally with salt and pepper, and set aside.

In a large bowl, whisk together the mayonnaise, sour cream, mustard, paprika, and egg until smooth. Add the chicken to the mixture and toss to coat. Set aside.

In a large skillet, heat the oil over medium heat until it begins to shimmer, 2 minutes. Add the breadcrumbs, stirring constantly, until golden brown, about 5 minutes. Remove the skillet from the heat and let cool for at least 5 minutes.

Using tongs, remove a chicken strip from the mayonnaise mixture and shake off any excess liquid. Place it in the breadcrumbs, pressing it gently and turning to make sure it is coated evenly all over, then place it on the cooling rack. Repeat with the remaining chicken strips until they're all coated.

Bake the chicken tenders in the oven until cooked through, about 15 minutes. Let them cool for 5 minutes and serve with the ranch.

Crudités

with Greek Yogurt Ranch

MAKES 8 TO 10 SERVINGS

If there's an art to making a cheese board, there's definitely a science behind the ideal crudités platter. Consider the old wedding adage: something raw, something charred, something pickled, and something crunchy. Upgrade the boring classics with pickled candy-stripe beets, Castelfranco radicchio (a pink-speckled vegetable that's more blossoming rose than bitter chicory), watermelon radishes, and rainbow carrots. Tie it all together with Greek Yogurt Ranch, a highly refreshing variation that matches the vegetal vibe of the whole scenario.

ingredients

For the pickles:
2 teaspoons coriander seeds
1 cup dill sprigs
3 medium carrots, peeled and cut into
  4-inch sticks
2 candy-stripe beets, peeled and cut into
  2-inch sticks
Kosher salt
1½ cups apple cider vinegar
1 tablespoon granulated sugar

For the charred vegetables:
8 tablespoons extra-virgin olive oil
½ pound broccolini, trimmed and thicker
  stalks cut lengthwise
Kosher salt
1 bunch radishes, trimmed and halved
  lengthwise
1 large fennel bulb, trimmed, tough outer
  layers removed, and quartered
  lengthwise

For assembly:
1 head chicory such as Castelfranco
  radicchio, stemmed and leaves separated
3 Persian cucumbers, trimmed and cut into
  4-inch sticks
Juice from ½ lemon
Extra-virgin olive oil, for drizzling
3½ cups Greek Yogurt Ranch (page 34),
  for serving

directions

Make the pickles: Divide the coriander seeds and dill sprigs evenly among 2 containers with airtight lids (such as mason jars). Place the carrots in 1 container and the beets in the other. Add a generous pinch of salt to each jar. In a medium bowl, whisk together the vinegar, ½ cup water, and sugar until the sugar dissolves. Pour the pickling liquid evenly over the carrots and beets. Cover and refrigerate for at least 24 hours or up to 5 days before serving.

Make the charred vegetables: In a large cast-iron skillet, heat 2½ tablespoons oil over medium-high heat. Add the broccolini and cook until tender and lightly charred, 1 to 2 minutes on each side. Season with salt. Remove the broccolini from the heat. Repeat with the remaining 5½ tablespoons oil, and the radishes and fennel.

Assemble the crudités platter: Arrange the pickled carrots and beets, charred vegetables, chicory leaves, and cucumbers on a large platter. Squeeze the lemon juice over the vegetables, and lightly drizzle them with some oil. Serve them alongside the ranch.

Mozzarella Sticks

with Labneh & Za'atar Ranch

Marinara sauce is nothing compared to mozz sticks' one true pairing, a tangy labneh ranch that means dipping fried cheese into more cheese. And with ranch seasoning mixed into the breading mixture, you get a bonus layer of ranch flavor after the initial thrill of the dip wears off. These can be assembled and kept in a resealable bag in the freezer up to a week ahead of time, so that a midnight snack is ready when you are.

ingredients

¾ cup all-purpose flour

3 large eggs

3 tablespoons buttermilk

2 cups panko breadcrumbs

1 tablespoon Homemade Ranch Seasoning (page 38) or store-bought ranch seasoning

1½ teaspoons dried parsley

1½ teaspoons dried dill

1 teaspoon dried oregano

1 pound mozzarella, cut into pieces 3 inches long and ¾-inch thick

Canola oil, for frying

Kosher salt

Labneh & Za'atar Ranch (page 32), for serving

directions

Line a rimmed baking sheet with parchment paper. Grab 3 medium shallow dishes. Place the flour in the first dish; whisk together the eggs and buttermilk in the second dish; combine the breadcrumbs, ranch seasoning, parsley, dill, and oregano in the third dish.

Dredge 1 piece of mozzarella in flour, making sure it's well coated and shaking off any excess. Dip the mozzarella in the egg mixture, letting the excess liquid drip off; then coat the mozzarella in the panko mixture, pressing gently to coat well. Transfer to the lined baking sheet and repeat with the remaining mozzarella pieces. Freeze for at least 2 hours.

In a large saucepan, heat 2 inches of oil over medium heat until an instant-read thermometer reads 350°F. Working in batches (don't overcrowd the pan), fry the mozzarella sticks until golden brown all over, 2 to 3 minutes. Transfer to a paper towel–lined plate and season with salt while still warm. Serve with the ranch.

Pizza

with Classic Ranch

MAKES 2 (10-INCH) PIZZAS

I know how easy it is to call in a pizza for delivery. You don't even have to talk to anyone now, you just press a few buttons on your phone, and it shows up in 30 minutes. But it's ridiculously simple to make at home. All you need is a cast-iron pan—no fancy pizza stone required—*and* you'll have a finished product that's actually hot, in half the time.

Now that you're sold on homemade pizza, do it right by adding ranch. The Internet is one giant platform for a ranch-on-pizza debate, with opinions ranging from "it's the pairing of a lifetime" to "please hand in your human card and go home." But the fact that it's made its way onto pizza menus from local dives to national megachains, speaks for itself. Topping it with a Marinara Ranch that uses herbs you'd find in normal bottled sauce and incorporates ranch for a creamy vodka sauce–like consistency makes for a pie you won't find in your local pizza shop. A generous drizzle of Classic Ranch is the crucial finishing touch—with more for dipping the crust into, of course.

ingredients

All-purpose flour, for dusting

22 ounces store-bought pizza dough at room temperature, halved

6 tablespoons extra-virgin olive oil, plus more for serving

1½ cups Marinara Ranch (page 42) or store-bought marinara sauce

1 pound low-moisture mozzarella cheese, grated

Toppings like roasted tomatoes, arugula, pepperoni, or other

Fresh basil leaves, for garnish

Finely grated Parmesan cheese, for serving

Classic Ranch (page 28) or store-bought ranch dressing, for serving

directions

Place an oven rack in the middle position and preheat the oven to 500°F (or as high as the oven will go). Place a 10-inch cast-iron skillet in the oven and let it get hot.

Lightly flour a clean work surface and stretch out 1 of the pieces of dough to a 10-inch round. Carefully remove the hot skillet from the oven and add 2 tablespoons oil, swirling the skillet to evenly coat it. Place the dough in the oiled skillet and brush it lightly with 1 tablespoon oil. Top the dough with half the marinara sauce, using the back of a measuring cup or spoon to spread the sauce evenly to the edges. Scatter half the mozzarella all over, adding other toppings as desired.

Place the skillet back in the oven and bake the pizza until the bottom of the crust is golden brown and the cheese is melted and bubbling, 12 to 15 minutes. Transfer the pizza to a cutting board and let it rest for 5 minutes. Repeat with the remaining ingredients to make a second pizza.

Drizzle the pizzas with more oil and top with the basil leaves and the Parmesan. Serve with the ranch.

Potato Skins

with Sour Cream Ranch

Instead of topping these little boats and their cheese-bacon cargo with a plain sour cream drizzle, channel TGI Fridays and serve them with a creamy ranch-flavored dip. The potato skins themselves are also amped up with ranch seasoning, because if you're going in on a plate of potato skins, "moderation" isn't in your vocabulary.

ingredients

4 russet potatoes, scrubbed
3 tablespoons extra-virgin olive oil
1½ cups grated cheddar cheese
2 teaspoons Homemade Ranch Seasoning
   (page 38) or store-bought ranch
   seasoning
¼ teaspoon paprika
Kosher salt
8 bacon slices, fried to a crisp and
   crumbled
Sour Cream Ranch (page 37), for serving
2 scallions, finely chopped, for garnish

directions

Preheat the oven to 400°F. Using a fork, prick the potatoes all over. Place them on a large rimmed baking sheet and brush all over with 1½ tablespoons of the oil. Roast until the potatoes are fork-tender, about 40 minutes. Remove the potatoes and allow to cool.

Meanwhile, in a bowl, combine the cheese, ranch seasoning, and paprika. Set aside. Once the potatoes are cool enough to handle, cut the potatoes in half lengthwise. Scoop out the flesh leaving a ¼-inch shell (discard the flesh or save for another use). Brush the outside and the inside of the potatoes with the remaining 1½ tablespoons oil. Place the potatoes cut side down on the baking sheet and roast until the skin side blisters slightly, about 8 minutes. Flip the potatoes over and lightly sprinkle them with salt. Return the potatoes to the oven and roast until the cut side turns golden brown, about 8 minutes more.

Remove the potato skins from the oven. Divide the cheese mixture and bacon crumbles evenly among the potato skins. Return them to the oven and roast until the cheese melts, about 4 minutes.

When ready to serve, top the potato skins with ranch and sprinkle with the scallions.

Freezer Burn: Ranch Ice Cream

There's no dessert chapter in this book, and that was not an accident. There's a time and a place for ranch dressing—which I firmly believe is a whenever, wherever situation, à la Shakira circa 2001—but I'm fine keeping my chocolate bar away from my bottle of ranch. A separation of church and state, if you will.

But some chefs have taken it upon themselves to turn ranch into ice cream, taking the "dairy" component perhaps too literally. On her award-winning TV show *A Chef's Life*, Vivian Howard makes fried okra with ranch ice cream in an attempt to convert okra haters. Being the admirable chef that she is, she knows that the process of getting someone to like something includes (a) frying it and (b) serving it with ranch.

You'll find a bona fide dessert ranch ice cream at Little Baby's in Philadelphia, where cofounder and owner Pete Angevine calls it, "Hilarious! Confusing! Just like ranch dressing, but cold!" It's made by adding buttermilk, dill, chives, garlic powder, onion powder, salt, and pepper to a grass-fed milk and cream base, and Angevine finds joy in watching people try it for the first time. "Like all great art, this ice cream flavor is divisive," he says. But true fans stand on the right side of that divide, because ranch lovers know a good thing when they see it. Little Baby's also makes pizza ice cream, so you can just combine the two and skip the whole act of chewing your food altogether.

It's a similar story at Sweet Peaks Ice Cream in Montana, where ranch ice cream is made with Hidden Valley Ranch seasoning and comes with carrots on the side. "It tastes just like ranch but extremely chilly," cofounder Marissa Keenan says.

Potato chips or Doritos are not unheard of swirled into artisanal ice cream, and Sweet Peaks also makes avocado toast ice cream. You can even find Cheetos soft serve in New York. Ranch paved the way for this, so know that nothing is impossible.

In this chapter, you'll find . . .

Snack Time

Now that you've mastered the basic recipes and know how to fancy up chicken wings, it's time to graduate to another genre of ranch-flavored goods—snacks, which also happen to be the best part(s) of any day.

Think of these as prepackaged foods that you can make yourself. Cool Ranch Doritos, packaged in one of the most recognizable chip bags we have, surely can't be labeled as "junk" food. A homemade version of them, though, is a good way to make you feel like you've done something with your day other than just sit on the couch with a bag of chips. Here, you'll start experimenting with ranch dust, which you can simply douse on popcorn—or do anything with from create a crispy coating on arancini to spice up Spam musubi.

Ranch-Dusted Popcorn

I have a love-hate relationship with white cheddar popcorn. It sounds like it should be a perfect union of two individually excellent things, but its artificial aftertaste ends up making it fall flat. Ranch popcorn effectively manages to fill the hole in my heart left by that disappointment. Nutritional yeast adds a cheesy taste to the popcorn without adding actual cheese, just like sprinkling homemade popcorn with ranch seasoning makes it taste like ranch without pouring dressing all over it.

ingredients

3 tablespoons coconut oil
⅓ cup popcorn kernels
3 tablespoons extra-virgin olive oil
1 tablespoon nutritional yeast
1 tablespoon Homemade Ranch Seasoning
  (page 38) or store-bought ranch
  seasoning, plus more to taste
Kosher salt

directions

In a large pot, heat the coconut oil over medium-high heat until it begins to shimmer. Add the popcorn kernels, shaking the pot so that the kernels are coated all over with oil. Cover and cook for about 3 to 5 minutes, shaking the pot often, until almost all the kernels have popped. The sound of popping will begin to slow down, and when you only hear a pop every 5 seconds, remove the pot from the heat and transfer the popcorn to a large bowl.

Drizzle the olive oil all over the popcorn and add the nutritional yeast and ranch seasoning. Toss well to coat. Season to taste with salt and more ranch seasoning, and serve immediately.

Ranch-Flavored Chex Mix

There are as many possible Chex mix variations as there are cat videos on YouTube. Maybe even more. But this one, with its cereal trifecta, heavy dose of ranch seasoning, and three forms of heat, takes the prize. For a sweet and savory version, add a handful of chopped dried fruit or mini chocolate chips after baking.

ingredients

3 cups Corn Chex

2 cups Rice Chex

2 cups Wheat Chex

2 cups mini pretzels

1 cup smoked almonds

1 cup cashews

1 cup pecans

2 cups garlic-flavored bite-size bagel chips, such as Gardetto's

½ cup (1 stick) unsalted butter, melted

2 teaspoons cayenne

¼ cup Homemade Ranch Seasoning (page 38) or store-bought ranch seasoning

1 tablespoon Aleppo pepper

1 tablespoon Worcestershire sauce

1 tablespoon Tabasco, or other hot sauce

6 garlic cloves, crushed

3 fresh thyme sprigs

directions

Preheat the oven to 250°F. In a large bowl, combine the Corn Chex, Rice Chex, Wheat Chex, pretzels, almonds, cashews, pecans, and bagel chips. In a small bowl, whisk together the butter, cayenne, ranch seasoning, pepper, Worcestershire, and Tabasco. Add the butter mixture, garlic, and thyme sprigs to the Chex mixture. Using a rubber spatula, stir the Chex mixture until evenly coated.

Divide the Chex mixture between 2 medium rimmed baking sheets, and spread evenly in a single layer. Bake, stirring every 15 minutes and turning baking sheets around halfway through, until the Chex mix is dry, fragrant, and toasted throughout, about 50 minutes.

Remove the Chex mix from the oven and discard the garlic cloves and thyme sprigs. Chex mix will keep in an airtight container at room temperature for up to 1 week. Gently rewarm in a 250°F oven before serving.

Ranch-Flavored Tortilla Chips

There are approximately 36 ingredients in Cool Ranch Doritos, 37 if you count "magic." But this six-ingredient version inspired by the iconic chip is a solid homemade interpretation. Paprika and tomato powder help capture that unmistakable whiff of the bag's essence you get upon first opening it. Plus, who knew making tortilla chips at home is almost easier than buying them (I said almost).

ingredients

¼ cup Homemade Ranch Seasoning (page 38) or store-bought ranch reasoning, plus more to taste
2 teaspoons paprika
2 teaspoons tomato powder
Canola oil, for frying
10 (6-inch) corn tortillas, cut into 6 triangles each
Kosher salt

directions

In a large bowl, whisk together the ranch seasoning, paprika, and tomato powder. Set aside.

In a heavy-bottomed pot, heat 2 inches of oil over medium heat until an instant-read thermometer reads 350°F (make sure you maintain the temperature of the oil during frying). Meanwhile, line a rimmed baking sheet with several layers of paper towels and set aside.

Working in batches (don't overcrowd the pot), fry all the tortilla pieces, turning occasionally, until golden brown and crisp, about 2 to 3 minutes per batch. Using a slotted spoon, transfer the tortilla chips to the lined baking sheet. Lightly sprinkle the chips with the seasoning mixture.

Transfer the tortilla chips to a large bowl and toss with some more ranch seasoning to coat completely. Sprinkle with salt to taste and serve immediately.

Elotes with Ranch Cotija

Elote is a classic Mexican street food and an unparalleled way to serve corn on the cob—grilled to perfection and slathered with sauce. It's also a great go-to for a summer gathering, making possible the classic party game of "Let's See Who Can Get the Most Mayo All Over Their Face." Spiking the already creamy sauce with ranch seasoning, as well as ranchifying the cheese that gets crumbled over the top, can only make this mess better. If you can't find cotija, sub in a crumbly cheese like ricotta salata for similar effect.

ingredients

Vegetable oil, for brushing
¼ cup mayonnaise
Juice from ½ lime, plus 4 wedges for
   serving
½ teaspoon chili powder
½ teaspoon cayenne
2 teaspoons Homemade Ranch Seasoning
   (page 38) or store-bought ranch
   seasoning
½ cup cotija cheese, crumbled
4 medium ears corn, husked
Kosher salt
Chopped cilantro, for garnish

directions

Brush the grates of a gas or charcoal grill with oil and heat it to medium-high heat.

In a small bowl, combine the mayonnaise, lime juice, chili powder, cayenne, and 1 teaspoon ranch seasoning. Set aside. In a separate small bowl, combine the cotija cheese and the remaining 1 teaspoon ranch seasoning.

Place the corn on the grill and roast, turning occasionally, until the corn is cooked through and charred in spots, about 10 minutes. Transfer it to a plate and brush each ear with the mayonnaise mixture (alternatively, you can pour the mayonnaise mixture over the corn). Season the corn lightly with salt. Sprinkle the cotija mixture and cilantro over the corn. Serve with the lime wedges.

Ranch Chicken Nachos with Ranch Crema

Mexican crema is a dairy product that's combined with poblano peppers for *rajas con crema*, spread in a torta, used as a finishing touch for tacos, and everything in between. It's thinner, tangier, and saltier than sour cream, but it lends itself just as well to mingling with ranch dressing on top of a tray of highly loaded nachos.

The ingredient list for these homemade nachos may seem hefty, but most parts can be prepared a day ahead of time and everything comes together quickly for the grand finale. Besides, no one likes a sparsely populated nacho plate. And this is coming from someone whose daily after-school snack was a plate of tortilla chips topped with pre-shredded cheese, microwaved for 32 seconds for a dish I thought was called "nachos." Speaking of tortilla chips: If you want to take both a bottom-up and top-down ranch approach here, use the Ranch-Flavored Tortilla Chips instead of the normal kind.

ingredients

For the ranch chicken:

2 boneless, skinless chicken breasts
1 (12-ounce) bottled beer
½ jalapeño, stemmed and roughly
   chopped
4 cilantro sprigs
Kosher salt
2 teaspoons garlic powder
2 teaspoons onion powder
2 teaspoons Aleppo pepper or
   1 teaspoon crushed red chile flakes
Juice from ½ lime, plus more to taste

For the ranch crema:

½ cup crema
¼ cup Classic Ranch (page 28) or
   store-bought ranch dressing
Juice from ½ lime
½ teaspoon garlic powder
½ teaspoon onion powder

For the pico de gallo:

3 plum tomatoes, chopped
½ white onion, chopped
1 jalapeño, stemmed, seeded, and
   chopped
1 tablespoon apple cider vinegar
½ cup chopped fresh cilantro

directions

Make the chicken: Place the chicken in a medium saucepan over medium heat and add the beer, jalapeño, cilantro, and 2 teaspoons salt. Add water if the chicken is not completely covered by the beer. Bring to a boil and simmer until cooked through, about 10 to 12 minutes. Allow the chicken to rest in the cooking liquid.

Once the chicken is cool enough to handle, shred it using 2 forks. In a medium bowl, combine the shredded chicken, garlic powder, onion powder, pepper, and lime juice. Toss to combine and season to taste with more salt and lime juice. Set aside.

Make the ranch crema: In a small bowl, combine the crema, ranch, lime juice, garlic powder, and onion powder. Cover and refrigerate for at least 20 minutes, allowing the flavors to come together. The ranch crema can be made up to 1 day ahead of time and kept in an airtight container in the refrigerator.

Make the pico de gallo: In a medium bowl, combine the tomatoes, onion, jalapeño, vinegar, and cilantro. Season to taste with salt and pepper. Allow the pico de gallo to sit at room temperature for at least 1 hour before serving.

Make the beans: In a small saucepan, heat the oil over medium heat. Add the beans, garlic, cumin, and coriander. Add a ½ cup water and bring to a simmer.

Kosher salt
Freshly ground black pepper

For the black beans:
1 tablespoon vegetable oil
1 (15-ounce) can black beans, drained and
 rinsed
1 garlic clove, minced
1 teaspoon ground cumin
1 teaspoon ground coriander
Kosher salt

For the assembly:
1 ripe Hass avocado, diced
Juice from ½ lime
Kosher salt
1 jalapeño, stemmed and thinly sliced
2 handfuls thick-cut tortilla chips or Ranch-
 Flavored Tortilla Chips (page 100)
1½ cups shredded cheddar cheese
1½ cups shredded Monterey Jack cheese
2 radishes, trimmed and thinly sliced
 (preferably on a mandoline)
Torn fresh cilantro leaves, for garnish

Season to taste with salt and cook until the liquid evaporates, about 10 minutes. The beans can be made up to 1 day ahead of time and kept in an airtight container in the refrigerator. Allow to come to room temperature before adding to nachos.

Assemble the nachos: Preheat the oven to 425°F, and line a large rimmed baking sheet with aluminum foil.

In a small bowl, combine the avocado and lime juice. Season with salt and toss to combine. Set aside. In a separate small bowl, cover the jalapeños with cold water. Take the jalapeño out of the water right before adding to the nachos.

Spread half the tortilla chips evenly on the lined baking sheet. Top with half the chicken, beans, and half of the cheddar and Monterey Jack. Repeat by layering with the remaining chips, chicken, beans, and cheese. Bake until the cheese is melted, bubbling, and beginning to brown in a few spots, about 6 minutes.

Transfer the nachos to a platter and top with the pico de gallo, avocado, jalapeño, and radishes. Spoon the ranch crema all over, add the cilantro, and serve.

Potato Salad with Ranch Rémoulade

Rémoulade is one of those recipes that makes you stop and wonder how it could possibly come together into something edible. Basically, every condiment is present here—mayonnaise, ketchup, mustard, baby pickles, horseradish, hot sauce—so it's only natural that ranch should show up to the party, too. Though French in origin, rémoulade is often used as a sauce in Southern cooking, which is why hot sauce and ketchup made their way in. Potatoes are a great neutral way to balance all that flavor.

ingredients

For the ranch rémoulade:

½ cup mayonnaise

1 teaspoon paprika

2 tablespoons chopped cornichons

1 garlic clove, minced

1 teaspoon prepared horseradish, like Gold's

1 teaspoon Tabasco, or other hot sauce

1 tablespoon Homemade Ranch Seasoning (page 38) or store-bought ranch seasoning

2 teaspoons fresh lemon juice

1 tablespoon chopped chives, plus more for garnish

1 teaspoon ketchup

1 teaspoon whole grain mustard

Kosher salt

Freshly ground black pepper

For the potato salad:

3 large eggs

2 pounds new potatoes, or small Yukon potatoes, quartered

¼ cup extra-virgin olive oil

Kosher salt

Freshly ground black pepper

¼ cup chopped fresh parsley, plus more for garnish

¼ cup chopped fresh dill

3 tablespoons chopped fresh mint

directions

Make the rémoulade: In a small bowl, combine the mayonnaise, paprika, cornichons, garlic, horseradish, Tabasco, ranch seasoning, lemon juice, chives, ketchup, and mustard. Season to taste with salt and pepper. Cover and refrigerate for at least 30 minutes. Ranch rémoulade can be made 3 days ahead of time and kept in an airtight container in the refrigerator.

Make the potato salad: Preheat the oven to 425°F. Fill a large bowl with cold water and ice, and set aside. Fill a medium saucepan with water and bring to a boil. Add the eggs and cook for 10 minutes. Using a slotted spoon, remove the eggs and immediately transfer them to the ice bath. Let them cool completely, peel them, and give them a rough chop.

Meanwhile, divide the potatoes and oil among 2 rimmed baking sheets. Season with salt and pepper, and toss to coat. Roast the potatoes, tossing halfway through, until golden brown and crisp, about 25 minutes. Let cool slightly.

In a large bowl, combine the roasted potatoes, eggs, rémoulade, parsley, dill, and mint. Garnish with the chives and parsley and serve immediately.

Ranch-Battered Onion Rings

These onion rings get the triple ranch treatment, which sounds like a luxury spa experience in Cabo you'd have to book months in advance, but is really just one allium's adventure through a lot of buttermilk. Start by soaking thick-cut onion rings in straight-up ranch, then you dip them in a ranch-seasoned batter before frying, and serve them with even more ranch dressing because, well, you might as well.

ingredients

1 large onion, cut into ½-inch thick slices and separated into individual rings

2 cups Classic Ranch (page 28) or store-bought ranch dressing, plus more for serving

1 cup all-purpose flour

½ cup cornstarch

1¼ teaspoons baking powder

Kosher salt, plus more to taste

½ teaspoon paprika

2 tablespoons Homemade Ranch Seasoning (page 38) or store-bought ranch seasoning

1½ cups club soda, chilled

Canola oil, for frying

directions

In a large bowl, combine the onion rings and cover them with the ranch dressing, tossing to coat them all over. Cover the bowl and refrigerate for at least 30 minutes (onion rings can be chilled up to 2 hours ahead of time).

Meanwhile, in a large bowl, whisk together the flour, cornstarch, baking powder, 1 teaspoon salt, paprika, and ranch seasoning. Slowly add the club soda in a steady stream, whisking constantly, until the batter is smooth. Set aside.

Place a cooling rack over a paper towel–lined baking sheet. In a large pot, heat 2 inches of oil over medium heat until an instant-read thermometer reads 350°F. Working in batches (don't overcrowd the pot), remove the onion rings from the ranch dressing letting the excess liquid drip off, then dredge them in the flour mixture, shaking off any excess. Fry, turning occasionally, until the onion rings are puffed and golden brown, about 2 minutes. Transfer the onion rings to the lined baking sheet. Season with salt while still warm. Repeat with the remaining onion rings.

Serve with more of the ranch.

Ranch Biscuits

Biscuits are the perfect recipe to debut Ranch Compound Butter. You'll use a whole stick of it in the biscuit dough itself, which comes together thanks to a buttermilk-ranch mixture. But the real pro move is to also slather the biscuits with it before drizzling them with some honey. Make sure the butter is as cold as possible when making the biscuits, as that's the key to getting them to be the fluffiest, flakiest version of themselves.

ingredients

½ cup (1 stick) frozen Ranch Compound Butter (page 39), plus more for serving

2 cups all-purpose flour, plus more for dusting

¼ teaspoon baking soda

1 tablespoon baking powder

½ cup buttermilk, plus 1 tablespoon for brushing

½ cup Classic Ranch (page 28) or store-bought ranch dressing

Honey, for serving (optional)

directions

Preheat the oven to 450°F. Line a rimmed baking sheet with parchment paper Using a box grater, grate the frozen ranch butter onto a small plate. Place the grated butter in the freezer for at least another 10 minutes. In a large bowl, mix together the flour, baking soda, and baking powder, and set aside. In a small bowl, whisk together the buttermilk and ranch. Set aside.

Remove the ranch butter from the freezer and add to the flour mixture. Using your fingers, incorporate the butter into the flour mixture, pinching the butter pieces into the flour until fully incorporated (be careful not to overmix the butter and flour; you want to avoid warming the butter too much with your hands). Using a rubber spatula, gently fold the buttermilk mixture into the dough, about 2 tablespoons at a time, making sure the buttermilk is fully incorporated before adding more (if you find it easier to use your hands, go for it). The goal is to add enough buttermilk for the dough to just come together.

Lightly dust a clean work surface with flour and place the dough on it. Using your hands, flatten the dough. Fold the dough in half onto itself and repeat this process 3 more times. Gently press down on the dough and flatten it into a 1-inch thick rectangle. Using a 3-inch circle cutter, cut the biscuits and transfer to the lined baking sheet, spacing the biscuits about 2 inches apart. Brush the tops with the remaining buttermilk. Bake until the tops are golden brown, 18 to 22 minutes.

Serve the biscuits with ranch butter and honey (if using).

Ranch Spam Musubi

MAKES 6 TO 8 SERVINGS

This Hawaiian-born snack is like a Spam sandwich, but instead of bread, slices of the canned meat are held together by rice and a nori sheet. It's often seasoned with *furikake*, a Japanese spice blend typically containing flavorful elements like dried fish, sesame seeds, and seaweed. But a liberal pinch of ranch seasoning in between the layers brings it even deeper down the snack rabbit hole. For best results, you'll want to spring for a musubi mold—a kitchen tool with low investment and high reward—but you can do without it by lining the empty Spam can with plastic wrap so that it hangs over the sides for easy removal, and using that to shape the rice.

ingredients

1 (12-ounce) can Spam

5 nori sheets, cut in half lengthwise

5 cups cooked sushi rice

2½ tablespoons Homemade Ranch Seasoning (page 38) or store-bought ranch seasoning, plus more for serving

2½ tablespoons furikake, plus more for serving

Special equipment: Musubi mold

directions

Turn the Spam onto its long side and cut it into ¼-inch slices, making about 8 pieces. Cook the Spam in a large nonstick skillet, flipping halfway through, until lightly crisped and browned on both sides, about 4 minutes. Remove from heat.

Working with 1 piece at a time, place the nori on a clean work surface with the short end toward you. Using your fingers, lightly moisten the nori with a little bit of water. Place the musubi maker in the middle of the nori sheet, perpendicular to it. The length of the musubi maker should fit the width of the nori sheet perfectly. Loosely fill the musubi maker with about a ¼ cup rice. Press down on the rice using the top of the musubi maker to create a flat rectangular rice base. Keeping the musubi maker in place, pull out the lid and lightly sprinkle a generous pinch of both the ranch seasoning and the furikake over the rice. Lay 1 cooked Spam slice over the rice. Sprinkle another generous pinch of ranch seasoning and furikake over the Spam. Top the Spam with another ¼ cup of rice and press on it with the musubi lid. You should get a perfectly rectangular, flat "sandwich." Remove the musubi maker carefully, and wrap both ends of the nori sheet over the top of the sandwich so that you get something that resembles a sushi roll. Repeat this process and create sandwiches from all of your Spam pieces, placing them under plastic wrap as they're being made. If the musubi maker begins to get sticky between rounds, wash it gently with warm water.

When ready to serve, use a serrated knife to cut each musubi sandwich into 1-inch thick pieces, like you would sushi. Lightly sprinkle each piece with more ranch seasoning and furikake. Serve immediately.

Ranch Grilled Cheese

Everyone has a trick that they swear makes the perfect, ultimate grilled cheese. Butter the bread, butter the pan, don't butter anything, put a teaspoon of butter behind your ear. But the mayo-on-bread move is one that actually yields a superior sandwich and is made even better by adding ranch seasoning to the mayonnaise pre-slather. Swap in provolone! Use whole wheat bread! Add ham! I don't care. Much like ranch on pizza, as long as you stick to the throuple of carbs, cheese, and ranch, you're in good hands.

ingredients

3½ tablespoons mayonnaise

4 teaspoons Homemade Ranch Seasoning (page 38) or store-bought ranch seasoning

4 (½-inch thick) slices pullman or sourdough bread

2 tablespoons unsalted butter

1½ cups grated sharp cheddar cheese

Classic Ranch (page 28) or store-bought ranch dressing, for serving

directions

In a small bowl, combine the mayonnaise with the ranch seasoning. Spread the ranch mayonnaise mixture on one side of each bread slice.

In a medium nonstick or cast-iron skillet, melt 1 tablespoon butter over medium heat. Place 2 bread slices mayonnaise-side down in the skillet. Divide the cheese evenly between the 2 slices. Top with the remaining 2 bread slices, mayonnaise-side up, gently pressing down on the slices with a spatula. Continue to fry the sandwiches until the bottoms are golden brown, 3 to 4 minutes. Using a spatula, flip the sandwiches. Add the remaining 1 tablespoon butter to the skillet and gently press down once again without smashing the sandwiches. Cook, rotating the skillet if necessary to allow for even browning, for another 3 to 4 minutes.

Transfer the sandwiches to a cutting board and let them rest briefly before cutting in half. Serve with a side of ranch.

Ranch Arancini

You know how some people keep preportioned balls of cookie dough in their freezer for when they have to host on a moment's notice? Do that, but with cheesy rice balls. These arancini have Classic Ranch built into the mixture, propped up by extra fresh herbs, and rolled in a ranch-seasoned breadcrumb combo before frying. You can make these ahead of time by transferring the baking sheet to the freezer once the arancini are shaped, then storing them in a plastic bag once they're completely frozen. They'll stay fresh there for about a month, and if no one stops by during that time, you get an arancini party for yourself. Worse things have happened.

ingredients

2 tablespoons unsalted butter

1 tablespoon extra-virgin olive oil

½ small red onion, finely chopped

3 cups chicken stock

1 cup Arborio rice

2 large eggs, beaten

½ cup finely grated parmesan

¼ cup chopped fresh chives, plus more for serving

3 tablespoons chopped fresh dill

¼ cup chopped fresh parsley

1 teaspoon finely grated lemon zest

1½ cups breadcrumbs

¼ cup Classic Ranch (page 28) or store-bought ranch dressing, plus more for serving

½ cup Homemade Ranch Seasoning (page 38) or store-bought ranch seasoning

½ cup grated provolone cheese

Canola oil, for frying

Kosher salt

Lemon wedges, for serving

directions

In a medium saucepan, combine the butter and olive oil over medium heat. Add the onion and cook until translucent and soft, about 5 minutes. Add the stock and bring to a boil. Add the rice and reduce the heat to a simmer. Cook the rice, stirring occasionally, until tender, 20 to 25 minutes. Transfer the rice to a parchment-lined rimmed baking sheet, spread it out in a thin layer, and allow to cool completely.

Place the cooled rice in a large bowl and add the eggs, parmesan, chives, dill, parsley, lemon zest, half the breadcrumbs, and ranch dressing. Stir well to combine. Measure about ¼ cup of the rice mixture and, using your hands, shape it into a ball. Place the rice ball on a parchment-lined baking sheet. Repeat with the remaining rice mixture. In a shallow dish, combine the ranch seasoning and the remaining breadcrumbs. Press your finger into the center of each rice ball, creating a small indent, and insert about 1 teaspoon provolone. Pinch the rice around the cheese to enclose and roll the balls in your hands to reshape. Roll the rice balls in the ranch breadcrumbs until evenly coated and return them to the parchment-lined baking sheet. Loosely cover with plastic wrap and transfer to the refrigerator. Chill for at least 1 hour or up to 1 day ahead of time.

In a large heavy-bottomed saucepan, heat 2 inches of canola oil over medium heat until an instant-read thermometer reads 350°F. Working in batches (don't overcrowd the pan), fry the rice balls, turning often, until golden brown and crisp all over, about 4 minutes. Using a slotted spoon, transfer the arancini to a paper towel–lined plate. Season with salt while the rice balls are still hot.

When ready to serve, sprinkle the arancini with chives, and serve with the lemon wedges and ranch.

Tapped Out:

Ranch Keg

They say you always remember your first keg. Mine was at a frat party in college (original), and in between figuring out what that pump thing actually did and calculating the ideal angle to hold my red cup up to the spout, I can confidently say there was one thing I wasn't thinking: "I wish this was filled with ranch dressing."

Turns out that not everyone was devoid of this thought, as in late 2017, Hidden Valley dropped a mini-keg bombshell on the world just in time for the holiday gifting season. They say it contains a lifetime supply of ranch, but it's only five liters, which sounds to me like they've either severely underestimated a human's lifespan or have been lying to us about serving sizes all this time.

It's not even 10 inches tall, making it the best possible way to decorate a table on a $50 budget. Let's just agree that you shouldn't attempt a keg stand here.

In this chapter, you'll find . . .

Old School Grub

Eating mac and cheese from your mom's kitchen counter while watching *Ren & Stimpy* or *Rocko's Modern Life* and wearing a plaid flannel shirt was practically a '90s rite of passage. Maybe this was a snack as you waited for dinner to cook (pork chops, probably), or you were trying to get out of eating a new recipe your dad was experimenting with (tamale pie, definitely).

We lived in a simpler time full of casseroles and pasta salads before kale took over our lives. It's time to give those staple meals of yesterday new life by way of ranch, another relic of the '90s, because (a) everything is better when you add ranch dressing, and (b) even comfort foods of yore can be made modern with a few twists. We've also moved past just ending a dish with a hit of ranch finesse—many of these recipes use ranch in three places, even four. Consider this a test of your true ranch devotion.

Ranch Mac and Cheese

In this recipe, you're making a roux that's thickened more with ranch seasoning than it is with flour, then turning it into béchamel—two fancy-sounding French culinary terms that almost make you forget about the fact that there's over a pound of cheese in this comforting childhood favorite. Feel free to substitute some of the cheddar or Gruyère with your favorite melty cheese, like fontina or Asiago.

ingredients

5 tablespoons unsalted butter, plus more for greasing

¾ cup panko breadcrumbs, plus more for finishing

¼ cup grated parmesan, plus more for sprinkling

Kosher salt

8 ounces dried medium shell pasta or medium elbow macaroni

1 cup whole milk

1 cup buttermilk

2 tablespoons all-purpose flour

3 tablespoons Homemade Ranch Seasoning (page 38), or store-bought ranch seasoning

½ pound sharp white cheddar cheese, grated

½ pound Gruyère cheese, grated

½ teaspoon mustard powder

Tabasco

Freshly ground black pepper

Chopped parsley, for garnish

directions

Preheat the oven to 400°F. In a large skillet, melt 2 tablespoons butter over medium heat. Add the breadcrumbs, stirring constantly, until golden brown, about 5 minutes. Transfer the breadcrumbs to a small bowl and add the parmesan, tossing to combine. Season with a pinch of salt and set aside.

In a large pot of salted boiling water, cook the pasta according to the package instructions until it is about 3 minutes shy of al dente. Drain it and set aside.

In a small saucepan, combine the milk and buttermilk, and bring to a bare simmer. Keep warm on low heat. Meanwhile, in a large saucepan, melt the remaining 3 tablespoon of butter over medium-low heat. Add the flour and ranch seasoning, whisking constantly, until smooth, about 1 minute. Add the buttermilk mixture a little at a time, whisking constantly, until the mixture has thickened, about 5 minutes. Remove from the heat and add almost all the grated cheddar and Gruyère (reserving a few handfuls for sprinkling over the top), mustard powder, and a few dashes of Tabasco. Stir to combine the sauce, then add in the pasta and season to taste with salt and pepper. Pour the cheesy pasta into a lightly greased 2-quart baking dish. Top with the remaining cheese and reserved breadcrumbs. Bake the pasta until the cheese is bubbling and the top is golden brown, 15 to 20 minutes. Let cool for at least 10 minutes.

Garnish with the chopped parsley before serving.

Ranch Pasta Salad

It's not a party unless ranch is invited, and it's not a picnic unless there's pasta salad on the menu. Combine those two golden rules, and you have a dish that makes a show out of cherry tomatoes and Kalamata olives from underneath a silky vinaigrette coating that uses Greek Yogurt Ranch. If you're really trying to prove a point, use the Homemade Ranch Pasta (page 162) instead of store-bought.

ingredients

For the vinaigrette:

1 large shallot, finely chopped

¼ cup red wine vinegar, plus more to taste

1 tablespoon Dijon mustard

1 tablespoon Homemade Ranch Seasoning (page 38) or store-bought ranch seasoning

½ cup extra-virgin olive oil

Kosher salt

Freshly ground black pepper

For the pasta salad:

4 cups cherry tomatoes

¼ cup extra-virgin olive oil, plus more for drizzling

Kosher salt

1 pound short dry pasta, such as bow tie, penne, casarecce, or fusilli

½ cup pitted Kalamata olives, roughly chopped

3 ounces feta, crumbled

2 large pickled peperoncini peppers, diced

1 cup fresh basil, roughly chopped

1 cup fresh mint, roughly chopped

1 cup Greek Yogurt Ranch (page 34)

2 tablespoons grated Pecorino-Romano cheese, plus more for sprinkling

Freshly ground black pepper

directions

Make the vinaigrette: In a small bowl, combine the shallot and vinegar. Add the mustard and ranch seasoning. In a steady stream, add the oil, whisking constantly, until the ingredients come together. Season to taste with salt and pepper, and set aside.

Make the pasta salad: Preheat the oven to 325°F. In a baking dish, toss the tomatoes with the oil until the tomatoes are well coated. Season with salt. Roast, tossing occasionally, until the tomatoes are nearly bursting and very tender, about 50 minutes. Set aside.

Meanwhile, in a large pot of boiling salted water, cook the pasta according to the package instructions until al dente. Drain the pasta and rinse with cold water. Transfer to a large bowl and lightly drizzle with oil, tossing to combine. Set aside.

Add the vinaigrette, roasted tomatoes, olives, feta, peppers, half the basil, half the mint, half the ranch, and the Pecorino-Romano. Toss to combine (the feta and ranch should lightly coat the pasta). Season to taste with salt, pepper, and more vinegar.

Transfer the pasta salad to a platter and top with the remaining basil and mint. Spoon dollops of the remaining ranch all over the pasta salad. Sprinkle with more Pecorino-Romano, drizzle oil all over, and serve.

Ranch Frittata with Feta, Chard, and Bacon

MAKES 4 SERVINGS

If you were alive and brunching anytime during the past four decades, you've likely encountered a frittata or two, and it's easy to see why they're so popular. This one relies entirely on fresh herbs for its ranch flavor, rather than the typical dry ones, and sources its dairy entirely from Greek yogurt, so as not to make it too soupy from buttermilk. The only requirement in this low-maintenance egg dish is that you pack those spoonfuls of herbs as tightly as you can before adding them to the yogurt, to maximize the ranch flavor.

ingredients

1 cup plain Greek yogurt

3 tablespoons finely chopped fresh chives, plus more for garnish

3 tablespoons finely chopped fresh parsley, plus extra leaves for garnish

2 tablespoons finely chopped fresh dill, plus extra leaves for garnish

1 garlic clove, minced

8 large eggs, beaten

⅓ cup crumbled feta

2 scallions, thinly sliced

Kosher salt

2 tablespoons extra-virgin olive oil

8 ounces slab bacon, thinly sliced and cut crosswise into ½-inch pieces

2 shallots, thinly sliced lengthwise

1 large bunch rainbow chard, stems removed and roughly chopped

1 teaspoon apple cider vinegar

directions

Preheat the oven to 400°F. In a small bowl, combine the yogurt, chives, parsley, dill, and garlic. In a medium bowl, combine half the yogurt mixture (reserve the other half), eggs, feta, scallions, and 1 tablespoon salt. Set aside.

In a medium cast-iron or nonstick skillet, heat the oil over medium heat. Add the bacon and cook, stirring often, until browned and crisp, about 7 minutes. Add the shallots and continue to cook, stirring often, until golden brown, about 5 minutes. Add the chard in batches, allowing each batch to wilt before adding another handful. Add the vinegar and stir to combine. Pour the egg mixture into the skillet. Cook, swirling the skillet occasionally to evenly distribute the egg, until the edges begin to set slightly, about 5 minutes. Transfer the skillet to the oven and bake until just set, about 15 minutes. When ready to serve, top the frittata with chives, parsley, and dill. Serve with the remaining yogurt mixture.

Loaded Sweet Potatoes

There is absolutely nothing that sweet potatoes can't do: You can slice them up for fries, mash them into a veggie burger base, and even puree and sweeten them to add to brownie batter. They're like the Little Engine That Could, except orange, and tubers. Loaded spuds are an old school, highly efficient way to turn an otherwise bland baked potato into a mountain of flavor and a meal in itself. They'll never truly go out of style, but the sweet potato swap and a double dose of ranch dip toppings—Ranch Guacamole and with Labneh & Za'atar Ranch—brings the dish into the 21st century.

ingredients

4 medium sweet potatoes (about 8 ounces each), scrubbed

2 tablespoons extra-virgin olive oil

½ cup (1 stick) Ranch Compound Butter (page 39), cut into cubes and softened

Kosher salt

Freshly ground black pepper

1 cup Labneh & Za'atar Ranch (page 32)

1 cup Ranch Guacamole (page 64)

1 cup grated Monterey Jack cheese

1 (15-ounce) can black beans, drained and rinsed

¼ cup sliced pepperoncini

Nutritional yeast, for sprinkling

½ cup chopped fresh cilantro

½ cup chopped scallions

Lime wedges, for serving

directions

Preheat the oven to 400°F. Line a rimmed baking sheet with parchment paper. Using a fork, prick the sweet potatoes all over. Rub the potatoes with oil and place them on the lined baking sheet. Roast the potatoes until fork-tender, about 45 minutes. Remove from heat and allow to cool slightly.

Once the potatoes are cool enough to handle, slice open each potato lengthwise, and scoop out most of the flesh. In a medium bowl, combine the potato flesh and the ranch butter, and season with salt and pepper. Lightly mash until well combined. Scoop the mashed potatoes back into their skins.

Top each potato with the labneh & za'atar ranch, ranch guacamole, cheese, black beans, and pepperoncini. Sprinkle some nutritional yeast, the cilantro, and scallions on top of each potato and serve with lime wedges.

Ranch-Loaded Breakfast Sandwich

Few things in this sandwich are spared ranch's influence. It finds its way into the eggs, biscuit, and sauce, making this a highly credible way to get away with eating ranch for breakfast. I would call this a hangover helper, but the ranch sriracha mayo will leave you drunk with pleasure, thus creating a vicious hungover cycle.

ingredients

1 strip thick-cut bacon, cut in half crosswise

1 tablespoon Ranch Compound Butter (page 39), softened

1 Ranch Biscuit (page 110), split in half

1 large egg

2 tablespoons Classic Ranch (page 28) or store-bought ranch dressing

Kosher salt

Freshly ground black pepper

1 teaspoon mayonnaise

1 teaspoon sriracha

1 slice (about 1 ounce) cheddar cheese

directions

Preheat the oven to 350°F. In a medium skillet, preferably cast iron, cook the bacon over medium heat until crisp and browned all over, 5 to 8 minutes. Transfer the bacon to a paper towel–lined plate and set aside.

Wipe the bacon grease out of the skillet, then melt the ranch butter over medium-high heat. Add each biscuit half to the skillet, cut-side down, and toast until golden brown, 3 to 5 minutes.

In a small bowl, whisk together the egg and 1 tablespoon ranch dressing until well combined. In a small nonstick skillet, fry the egg mixture over medium-low heat, gently pushing the edges of the egg inward with a rubber spatula and swirling the skillet to evenly distribute the egg (like you would with an omelet). Continue to push the edges without creating too many creases, until the egg is cooked around the edges and still slightly jiggly in the center, about 5 minutes. Fold the egg in half and then again into a quarter. Season with salt and pepper.

In a small bowl, combine the mayonnaise, sriracha, and remaining 1 tablespoon ranch. To assemble the sandwich, spread the ranch sriracha mayonnaise on the cut sides of the biscuit. Place the egg on the bottom half of the biscuit, followed by the cheese, and then the bacon. Top with the other half of the biscuit and place in the oven until the cheese melts, about 5 minutes. Serve immediately.

Mixed Lettuce Salad

with Green Goddess Ranch

Complement the classic California dressing with a salad that goes beyond the typical iceberg lettuce–cherry tomato situation, one with crunchy pepita seeds, sliced fennel, and cooling mint. Buttery Bibb, butter, or little gem lettuces are the perfect vessels for fun little pools of dressing, but you can sub in romaine hearts for more of a basic Caesar vibe.

ingredients

3 tablespoons vegetable oil
1 cup pepita seeds, plus more for garnish
¼ teaspoon Aleppo pepper or red chile
    flakes
Flaky sea salt
2 small lettuce heads, such as Bibb,
    butter, or little gem, stemmed and leaves
    separated
1 small head fennel, thinly sliced
    (preferably on a mandoline)
1 Persian cucumber, cut into ¼-inch slices
Juice from ½ lemon
¼ cup Green Goddess Ranch (page 46),
    plus more for serving
Fresh mint leaves, for garnish

directions

In a medium skillet, heat 1 tablespoon oil over medium heat. Add the pepita seeds, and cook, stirring often, until they are lightly browned and toasted, about 5 minutes. Remove from the heat and set aside to cool slightly.

In a food processor (or with a small mortar and pestle), combine the cooled pepita seeds, pepper, and a ¼ teaspoon flaky salt. Pulse, scraping down the sides often, until you get a chunky consistency.

In a large bowl, place the lettuce, fennel, cucumber, the remaining 2 tablespoons oil, and the lemon juice. Season with salt and toss to combine. Transfer the salad to a serving bowl. Spoon the ranch all over the salad. Garnish with more pepita seeds, some mint leaves, and more ranch.

Ranch Buttermilk Waffles

Quality of life increases proportionally to the number of frozen waffles stashed in your freezer. But no store-bought box can compete with freezing homemade ones and squirreling them away to delight a future version of yourself, especially when they're permeated with a ranch seasoning that plays up the buttermilk base. You end up with a savory waffle that works just as well for dinner as it does for breakfast, and can play host to anything from maple syrup to fried chicken or bacon. And, of course, Ranch Compound Butter (page 39) is always an option.

ingredients

½ cup (1 stick) unsalted butter, melted, plus more for serving

2 large eggs at room temperature, beaten

2 cups buttermilk

2 tablespoons brown sugar

2 teaspoons baking powder

1 teaspoon baking soda

2¼ cups all-purpose flour

3 tablespoons Homemade Ranch Seasoning (page 38) or store-bought ranch seasoning

1½ teaspoons kosher salt

Vegetable oil spray, for coating the waffle iron

Maple syrup, for serving

Special equipment: Waffle iron

directions

Preheat the oven to 250°F. In a medium bowl, whisk together the butter, eggs, and buttermilk. In a second medium bowl, whisk together the brown sugar, baking powder, baking soda, flour, ranch seasoning, and salt. Gradually add the dry ingredients to the wet ingredients, whisking constantly and scraping down the sides of the bowl as necessary, until the ingredients are well combined and the batter is nearly smooth (don't worry if a few lumps remain).

Spray the waffle iron with vegetable oil spray and fill it with batter (use about ⅓ cup of batter for an 8-inch round waffle). Cook the waffles according to the manufacturer's instructions until golden brown. Transfer the waffles to a rimmed baking sheet and keep warm in the oven until serving.

Serve the waffles with butter and maple syrup.

Ranch-Crusted Pork Chops

An aggressive marketing campaign by the National Pork Board in the 1980s advertised pork as "the other white meat," in an effort to make consumers lay off the chicken for a second and give pigs a chance. If that's true, then ranch seasoning is "the other dry rub." Don't get turned off by the addition of sugar to the mix—it helps create a crust that seals in all that ranch flavor, which is further amplified by cheesy Herbed Feta Ranch Dip, a welcome savory alternative to the usual applesauce side.

ingredients

4 teaspoons Homemade Ranch Seasoning (page 38) or store-bought ranch seasoning

½ teaspoon granulated sugar

Kosher salt

Freshly ground black pepper

4 (1-inch thick) bone-in pork chops (about 2 pounds), patted dry with paper towels

2 tablespoons vegetable oil

½ lemon

½ cup fresh parsley leaves with tender stems

Herbed Feta Ranch Dip (page 56), for serving

directions

In a small bowl, combine the ranch seasoning, sugar, 1 teaspoon salt, and ½ teaspoon pepper. Rub the pork chops all over with the dry seasoning and let them sit at room temperature for 10 minutes.

In a large skillet, preferably cast iron, heat the oil over medium-high heat until it begins to shimmer. Gently add the pork chops to the skillet and cook, swirling the pan occasionally, until the bottoms of the pork chops have developed a crust and become deeply browned, 4 to 6 minutes. Flip the chops over and cook for an additional minute over medium-low heat. Turn the heat off and allow the pork chops to rest in the skillet for about 10 minutes.

Transfer the pork chops to a plate and drizzle them all over with the pan juices. Squeeze the lemon half over the pork chops and serve with a salad of parsley leaves and herbed feta ranch dip.

Ranch Fried Chicken and Ranch Mashed Potatoes

MAKES 4 TO 6 SERVINGS

Buttermilk fried chicken is timeless. It's also just some herbs and spices away from being ranch fried chicken. To remedy this, ranch goes into the marinade and the flour mixture, so that it has all the right herbs in all the right places. The chicken is joined by some ranchified mashed potatoes for a well-rounded experience. Clearly, no one will be mad if Ranch Buttermilk Waffles (page 136) also make an appearance on this plate.

ingredients

For the mashed potatoes:

3 pounds Yukon Gold potatoes, peeled and quartered

Kosher salt

1½ cups whole milk

1 stick (8 tablespoons) Ranch Compound Butter (page 39)

½ cup Sour Cream Ranch (page 37)

2 tablespoons chopped fresh chives

For the fried chicken:

4 cups buttermilk

1 cup sour cream

3 garlic cloves, minced

Kosher salt

Freshly ground black pepper

2½ teaspoons onion powder

2 teaspoons garlic powder

¼ cup chopped fresh chives

¼ cup chopped fresh parsley

½ teaspoon Tabasco

Juice from 1 lemon

1 (3½- to 4-pound) whole chicken, cut into 8 pieces (wings, breasts, thighs, drumsticks)

Canola oil, for frying

2 cups all-purpose flour

3 tablespoons Homemade Ranch Seasoning (page 38) or store-bought ranch seasoning

Labneh & Za'atar Ranch (page 32), for serving

directions

Make the mashed potatoes: In a large saucepan, bring the potatoes to a boil in salty water. Lower the heat and simmer for about 10 to 12 minutes, until they are fork-tender.

Meanwhile, in a small saucepan, heat the milk and the ranch butter on low heat, until the butter has melted and the milk is warmed through, about 5 minutes. Set aside.

When the potatoes are done, drain and mash them with a potato masher, then slowly whisk in the butter and milk mixture, adding a little at a time until you reach the desired consistency. Fold in the ranch, season with salt, and stir until well combined. Transfer the potatoes to a serving bowl and top with chives.

Make the fried chicken: In a large bowl, whisk together the buttermilk, sour cream, garlic, 2 tablespoons salt, 2 teaspoons pepper, 1½ teaspoons onion powder, 1 teaspoon garlic powder, chives, parsley, Tabasco, and lemon juice. Add the chicken and toss to combine. Cover and refrigerate for at least 4 hours, or up to 12 hours.

Remove the chicken from the refrigerator and allow it to sit at room temperature for at least 30 minutes. In a large Dutch oven or a pot, heat 3 inches of oil over medium heat until an instant-read thermometer reads 350°F. While the oil is heating, in a large bowl, whisk together the flour, ranch seasoning, and the remaining 1 teaspoon onion powder and 1 teaspoon garlic powder. Place a cooling rack over a paper towel–lined baking sheet.

Working in batches, remove the chicken pieces from the marinade, allowing the excess liquid to drip off, dredge it in the flour mixture, and fry until dark golden brown and crispy, about 12 to 15 minutes. Using a slotted spoon, transfer the chicken to the cooling rack. Season with salt while the chicken is still warm. Repeat with the remaining chicken pieces.

Serve immediately with the mashed potatoes and a side of labneh & za'atar ranch for dipping.

Ranch Tamale Pie

Tamales are a Mexican dish, but when you shed the corn husk, put the filling in a cornbread crust, and label it "pie," it becomes an unmistakably American take on the classic version—even more so when you add ranch seasoning to that tender, tangy dough. You end up with a dish that's somewhat of a savory cobbler, served with cooling Greek Yogurt Ranch to balance the spice of the filling.

ingredients

4 tablespoons vegetable oil

4 garlic cloves, thinly sliced

1 medium onion, finely chopped

1 jalapeño, stemmed, seeded, and finely chopped

Kosher salt

1 pound ground beef

1 (15-ounce) can black beans, drained and rinsed

1 teaspoon ground cumin

1 teaspoon cayenne

Freshly ground black pepper

1 cup chicken stock or water

1 cup crushed tomatoes

1½ cups cornmeal

6 tablespoons all-purpose flour

2 tablespoons granulated sugar

8 teaspoons Homemade Ranch Seasoning (page 38) or store-bought ranch seasoning

2 teaspoons baking powder

2 large eggs

1½ cups grated Monterey Jack cheese

½ cup buttermilk

Fresh cilantro leaves with tender stems, for serving

Greek Yogurt Ranch (page 34), for serving

directions

Preheat the oven to 400°F. In a 10-inch cast-iron skillet or large ovenproof saucepan, heat 3 tablespoons oil over medium heat. Add the garlic, onion, and jalapeño. Season with salt and cook, stirring often, until the onion becomes golden brown, about 6 minutes. Add the beef and season liberally with salt. Using the back of a wooden spoon, break up the beef and cook, stirring often, until the beef begins to brown, 6 to 8 minutes. Add the beans, cumin, cayenne, a pinch of pepper, stock, and tomatoes, and stir to combine. Reduce the heat and simmer, stirring occasionally, until the liquid reduces by two-thirds, about 30 minutes. Remove from the heat and set aside.

In a medium bowl, whisk together the cornmeal, flour, sugar, ranch seasoning, and baking powder. In a separate small bowl, whisk together the eggs, cheese, buttermilk, and the remaining 1 tablespoon oil. Whisk the buttermilk mixture into the dry ingredients until well combined.

Dollop the batter over the chili and spread into an even top layer. Transfer the skillet to the oven. Bake until the top is golden brown, about 45 minutes. Cool slightly for at least 10 minutes.

Top with some cilantro and serve with a side of greek yogurt ranch, which you can spoon over the top of your slice.

Sipping Haterade:
The Naysayers

Even in a world that contains ranch-flavored soda and breath mints, something even more alarming exists: people who claim they don't like ranch dressing.

Where there's something beautiful, there will always be darkness lurking in the corner. That's why a Google search brings up various headlines from dissenters like "Ranch Dressing Is What's Wrong with America" and "6 Dangerous Salad Dressing Facts." It also gets you one titled "Using Ranch Dressing for Bongwater Is Bad, but Mouthwash Is Good," but we'll save that one for the sequel.

Unless it's been sitting unrefrigerated for seven years, salad dressing does not present an imminent danger. Until an innocent bottle of buttermilk and herbs grows the ability to pick up a taser and numb you into a daze, I think it's safe to say you'll be just fine from putting ranch on your food. Plus, few other things can please both the salad-eating camp and the only-beige-food type with such ease. Even Gwyneth Paltrow, who's gone on record that she would rather smoke crack than eat cheese from a can, has a recipe for ranch dressing in one of her cookbooks. Her use of Vegenaise may be questionable, but the Old Bay addition is highly commendable.

Everyone is more than entitled to their own opinions, it's just that some of those opinions are wrong. If a ranch hatred is born for health reasons, I'd like to know what these virtuous haters are eating for every meal. It's not like we're taking shots of the stuff as we eat our pizza . . . or not all of us, I suppose. A teaspoon of mayonnaise is not the apocalypse. If it's for taste reasons, I'll just assume you had one bad experience, and to that I propose a credo that you should try anything twice.

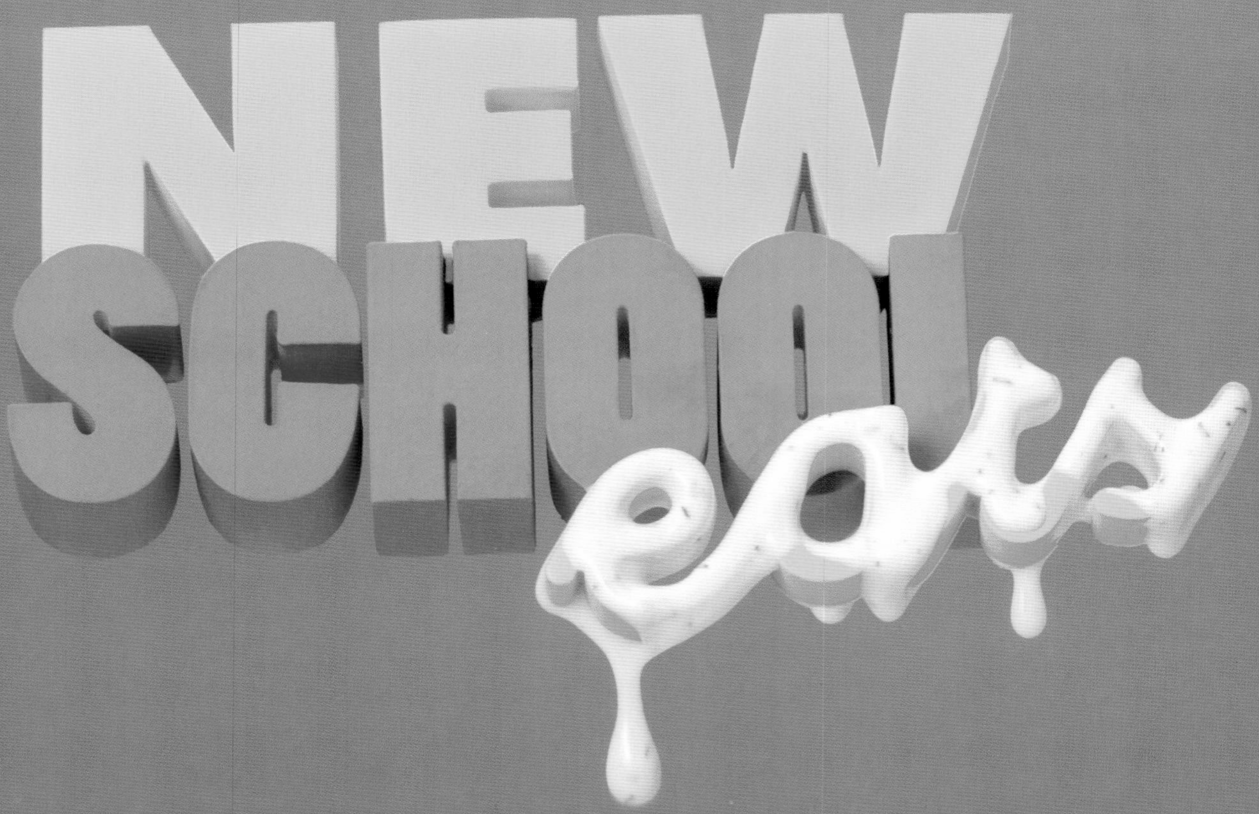
NEW
SCHOOL
eats

In this chapter, you'll find . . .

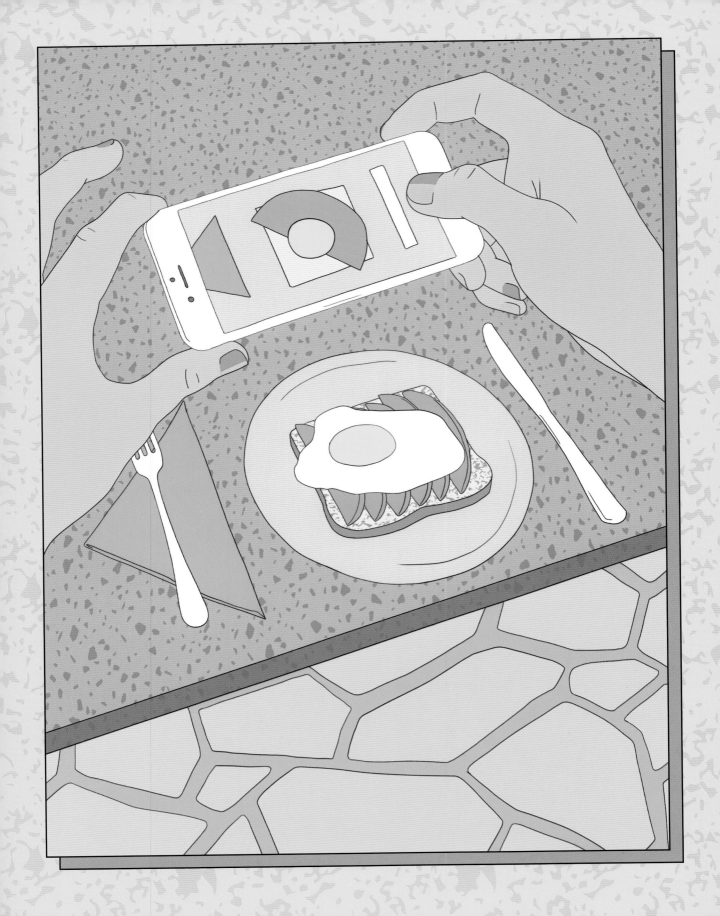

New School Eats

Now that you know how to dress up the classics and class up the snacks you binge on, it's time to step up and use ranch in even more out-of-the-box ways, like in a fragrant curry or as a marinade for lamb skewers. These are the dishes that would result if a bottle of ranch dressing walked into a small plates restaurant and spontaneously combusted all over everything in sight.

You'll notice more composed salads here, as well as green things in general, as a nod to the general trend toward the conscious plant-based efforts of the past decade. That's not to say we're not still delighting in a heavy pour of mayo-laden ranch, it just means we're finding a way to balance it with all our non-GMO shopping cart items and farmers' market hauls—which, in a way, is ranch returning to its salad roots. Despite this shift, ranch's fan base is stronger than ever. Chefs all over the country use ranch on their pizza, fries, and tacos, no matter how many Michelin stars their restaurants might have. And it's still the leading salad dressing in the United States, with a national consumer survey showing that it outmuscles the seemingly common vinaigrette nearly three to one.

Shaved Vegetable Flatbread with Ranch Tzatziki

MAKES 2 FLATBREADS

There's a pair of GPS coordinates in the center of the Venn diagram of salads, wraps, and pizzas where this dish lives, tethered to each by a ranch tzatziki that would work on all three. There's a lot of mandoline work to be done here, but you can make fast work of it once you get in the groove. Put on some music—you can find my "Mandoline" playlist on Spotify—and let loose . . . just watch your fingers.

ingredients

For the ranch tzatziki:
3 Persian cucumbers, finely chopped
Kosher salt
1 cup plain Greek yogurt
¼ cup sour cream
2 garlic cloves, minced
Juice from 1 lemon
¼ cup extra-virgin olive oil
¼ cup chopped fresh mint
3 tablespoons chopped fresh dill
3 tablespoons chopped fresh chives

For the shaved vegetable salad:
1 romaine heart, leaves separated and
    torn into large pieces
2 cups thinly shaved fennel
2 cups thinly shaved carrots
1 cup thinly shaved radishes
1 cup cherry tomatoes, halved
1 cup green olives, pitted and roughly
    chopped
Juice from 1 lemon
3 cups extra-virgin olive oil
2 tablespoons white wine vinegar
Kosher salt
Freshly ground black pepper

For assembly:
1 cup Ranch Hummus (page 62)
4 large flatbreads such as naan or pita,
    toasted or grilled
½ cup fresh parsley leaves with tender
    stems
½ cup fresh mint leaves, torn
Hot sauce, for serving

directions

Make the ranch tzatziki: In a small bowl, combine the cucumbers with a generous pinch of salt. Toss to combine and let sit for at least 30 minutes. Gently press on the cucumbers to expel any liquid, then drain. In a medium bowl, combine the cucumbers, yogurt, sour cream, garlic, lemon juice, and oil. Season to taste with more salt. Cover and refrigerate for at least 30 minutes or overnight. Stir in the mint, dill, and chives right before serving.

Make the shaved vegetable salad: In a large bowl, combine the romaine leaves, fennel, carrots, radishes, tomatoes, and olives. Add in the lemon juice, oil, and vinegar. Season liberally with salt and pepper. Toss to combine and set aside.

To assemble, divide and spread the ranch hummus over the flatbreads. Add the parsley and mint to the salad, and toss once to combine. Divide the salad evenly on top of the flatbreads. Spoon some tzatziki over the salad and serve with hot sauce and extra ranch tzatziki on the side.

Chickpea Fritters

with Coconut Cream & Shiso Ranch

You might see "chickpea" and "fritters" together and think falafel, but these are more like a legume-based latke or smashed veggie burger than anything else. Using coconut cream ranch in the batter makes for really juicy fritters. So that you'll top them with even more of that ranch just because you want to, not because you need the extra moisture.

ingredients

2 (15-ounce) cans chickpeas, drained and rinsed
½ small red onion, finely chopped
¼ cup all-purpose flour
1 tablespoon cornstarch
½ cup chopped cilantro
1 large egg, beaten
1 teaspoon ground coriander
1 teaspoon ground cumin
1 cup Coconut Cream & Shiso Ranch (page 31)
Kosher salt
Freshly ground black pepper
6 tablespoons vegetable oil
Salad greens, for serving
Lemon wedges, for serving

directions

In a food processor, combine the chickpeas, onion, flour, cornstarch, cilantro, egg, coriander, cumin, ¼ cup ranch, and a pinch of salt and pepper. Pulse, scraping down the sides occasionally, until the chickpeas begin to break down and a coarse paste begins to form. Adjust seasoning if necessary.

Line a rimmed baking sheet with parchment paper. Scoop out ¼ cup of the chickpea mixture at a time and roll into balls. Gently press on the chickpea balls to flatten into ½-inch-thick patties.

In a skillet, preferably cast iron or nonstick, heat 3 tablespoons of oil over medium heat until the oil is shimmering. Making sure not to overcrowd the pan, add half the chickpea fritters. Cook the fritters, flipping halfway through, until golden brown on both sides, about 10 minutes. Transfer the fritters to a paper towel–lined plate or baking sheet. Season with salt immediately while fritters are still warm. Add the remaining 3 tablespoons oil to the pan and repeat with the remaining fritters.

Serve the fritters with a bed of greens, alongside lemon wedges and the remaining ranch.

Snap Pea Salad

with Ricotta Ranch

This Italian-ish salad goes out to anyone who ever said ranch isn't a "health food." It's at once cooling from the mint, crisp from flash-cooked snap peas, spicy from the Calabrian chiles, and tangy from spoonfuls of Ricotta Ranch. There's also a ranch-based vinaigrette, proving that creamy dressing isn't the only liquid shape ranch can take.

ingredients

Kosher salt

1½ pounds sugar snap peas, trimmed, stringed, cut in half on a diagonal

¼ cup extra-virgin olive oil

2 tablespoons apple cider vinegar

1 teaspoon Dijon mustard

1 garlic clove, minced

1 tablespoon Classic Ranch (page 28) or store-bought ranch dressing

2 teaspoons chopped Calabrian chile peppers or 1 teaspoon Aleppo pepper or red chile flakes

3 radishes, thinly sliced (preferably on a mandoline)

Freshly ground black pepper

½ cup fresh mint leaves

¼ cup chopped fresh chives

1½ cups Ricotta Ranch (page 30)

directions

In a large bowl, combine ice and water to create an ice bath. In a large pot of salted boiling water, cook the snap peas until crisp and tender, about 2 minutes. Using a slotted spoon, immediately transfer the snap peas to the prepared ice bath. Let cool completely. Drain and pat the snap peas dry with paper towels.

In a large bowl, whisk together the oil, vinegar, mustard, garlic, classic ranch, and chiles until the ingredients come together. Add the snap peas and radishes. Season with salt and black pepper, and toss to combine.

When ready to serve, transfer the salad to a platter and top with the mint, chives, and ricotta ranch.

Summer Corn, Tomato, and Avocado Salad

with Classic Ranch

If you put all the best things about summer on a plate, added ranch dressing, and took out the beach—no one likes a sandy salad—this is what you'd end up with. Heirloom tomatoes and fresh corn are ideal, but substitute with cherry tomatoes and frozen kernels if you need a sunshine fix no matter the season.

ingredients

Vegetable oil, for brushing

6 ears of corn, shucked

5 tablespoons extra-virgin olive oil, plus more for brushing the grill

Kosher salt

Freshly ground black pepper

6 slices bacon

2 large heirloom tomatoes, chopped into 1-inch pieces

1 cup loosely packed basil leaves, larger leaves torn

¼ cup fresh lime juice

1 ripe Hass avocado, sliced

Chopped fresh chives, for garnish

1 cup Classic Ranch (page 28)

directions

Preheat a charcoal or gas grill to medium-high heat. Brush the grill grates with vegetable oil. Place the corn on a rimmed baking sheet and rub 1 tablespoon olive oil all over the corn. Season with salt and pepper. Grill the corn until cooked through and charred in some spots, about 10 minutes. Remove from the heat and let cool slightly. Once the corn is cool enough to handle, cut the kernels off of the cob.

In a large skillet, cook the bacon over medium heat, turning halfway through, until crisp all over, about 8 minutes. Transfer the bacon to a paper towel–lined plate. Crumble the bacon into ½-inch pieces. In a large bowl, combine the remaining 4 tablespoons olive oil, corn, bacon, tomatoes, ½ cup basil, lime juice, and avocado. Season to taste with more salt and pepper, and toss to combine.

When ready to serve, transfer the salad to a large bowl. Top with the remaining basil and some chives. Spoon the ranch all over the salad.

Quinoa Grain Bowl

with Turmeric Ranch

The always buzzy, sometimes filling grain bowl gets a revamp with quinoa, toasted almonds, ranch-flavored feta, and a sunny turmeric dressing to tie it all together. Make it vegan by swapping the Coconut Cream & Shiso Ranch (page 31) for the Turmeric Ranch and bypassing the Herbed Feta Ranch Dip and egg, or opt for Green Goddess Ranch (page 46) to release the true Californian in you.

ingredients

4 cups baby kale, stems removed and roughly chopped

1 tablespoon apple cider vinegar

Kosher salt

½ medium red onion, thinly sliced

Juice from 1 lemon

4 large eggs at room temperature

Freshly ground black pepper

2 cups cooked quinoa

1 (15-ounce) can chickpeas, drained and rinsed

1 ripe Hass avocado, sliced

½ cup toasted almonds, chopped

¼ cup Herbed Feta Ranch Dip (page 56)

2 medium radishes, thinly sliced lengthwise

Turmeric Ranch (page 44)

directions

In a large bowl, combine the kale and vinegar. Season with salt and gently massage the kale to incorporate the seasoning. Let the kale sit at room temperature for about 15 minutes.

In a small bowl, combine the onion and lemon juice, and season lightly with a pinch of salt. Allow the onion to macerate in the lemon juice for at least 15 minutes (the onion can macerate in lemon juice in an airtight container in the refrigerator overnight). Drain the onion before using, discarding the lemon juice.

In a medium saucepan, bring salted water to a simmer over medium-low heat. Crack the eggs into the water and poach until the whites are fully set, about 2 minutes. Transfer the eggs to a paper towel–lined plate and season with salt and pepper.

Evenly divide the quinoa among 4 bowls, and top with the kale, chickpeas, onion, avocado, almonds, herbed feta ranch dip, and radishes. Top each bowl with a poached egg. Drizzle some turmeric ranch over the top, and serve.

Ranch-Roasted Squash, Kale, and Bread Salad

A salad made out of bread is the best way to eat salad. Panzanella, the classic Italian summer salad consisting of bread, tomatoes, and basil, gets an autumnal treatment with squash and kale instead. The squash gets tossed with staple ranch spices for concentrated ranch power, but with its fresh herbs, macerated onions, and Ricotta Ranch, the whole thing is loaded with ranch characteristics to the core.

ingredients

1 teaspoon onion powder

1 teaspoon garlic powder

½ teaspoon sumac

½ teaspoon dried parsley

½ teaspoon dried dill

1 small (about 1½ pounds) butternut squash, peeled, seeded, and cut into 1-inch pieces

½ cup extra-virgin olive oil, plus more for serving

Kosher salt

½ small red onion, thinly sliced

3 tablespoons white wine vinegar, plus more for serving

½ medium loaf sourdough bread, torn into 1-inch pieces (about 6 cups)

1 medium bunch Tuscan kale, ribs and stems removed, leaves cut into 1-inch strips

Freshly ground black pepper

Juice from ½ lemon

1½ cups Ricotta Ranch (page 30)

1½ cups torn mixed fresh herbs such as dill, parsley, tarragon, or mint

directions

Preheat the oven to 400°F. In a small bowl, whisk together the onion powder, garlic powder, sumac, dried parsley, and dried dill. On a rimmed baking sheet, combine the squash, spice mixture, and 2 tablespoons oil. Season with salt and toss to coat. Spread the squash evenly in a single layer on the baking sheet and roast until fork-tender, 30 to 40 minutes. Let the squash cool slightly. Leave the oven on.

In a large bowl, combine the onion and the vinegar. Season with salt and let sit for at least 20 minutes. Add the roasted squash, toss to combine, and set aside.

Meanwhile, on a rimmed baking sheet, add 4 tablespoons oil, bread, and kale (divide between 2 baking sheets if it seems crowded). Season with salt and pepper. Bake, tossing once, until the bread is golden brown and the kale is slightly crisp, 8 to 10 minutes. Set aside and let cool slightly.

Add the bread and kale to the large bowl with the onion and squash. Drizzle with the remaining 2 tablespoons oil and squeeze the lemon juice all over. Season to taste with more salt and toss to combine. Set aside for a few minutes, allowing the flavors to come together.

When ready to serve, drizzle with more oil and vinegar. Dot the ranch all over and top with fresh herbs.

Homemade Ranch Pasta

In the age of boutique boxing classes and CrossFit gyms, you're more than physically equipped to knead that dough and make fresh pasta at home. Slice it into long strands, or just cut it into rectangles and use as lasagna sheets. Ranch seasoning goes into the dough with the salt, so that after you knead it (side note: free therapy!), no square millimeter of pasta gets left un-ranched.

ingredients

9 ounces all-purpose flour (about 2 cups), plus more for sprinkling

1 ounce (about 2 tablespoons) Homemade Ranch Seasoning (page 38) or store-bought ranch seasoning

Kosher salt

1 large egg plus the yolks from 4 large eggs

Special equipment: Pasta maker machine

directions

In a large bowl, combine the flour, ranch seasoning, and 1 teaspoon salt. On a clean lightly floured work surface, arrange the flour mixture into a pile. Make a well in the center and add the egg and the egg yolks. Using a fork, beat the eggs, gradually beating in the flour from the walls of the well. Continue to beat until a wet, sticky dough forms. Begin to fold the dough onto itself, rotating it a quarter turn every few seconds, and continue to knead until the dough becomes smooth and is no longer sticky (if the dough feels too wet, lightly sprinkle flour over it; if the dough feels too dry, add water using a spray bottle). Wrap the dough in plastic and let it rest for 30 minutes on the kitchen counter. The dough can be made a day ahead of time and kept wrapped tightly in plastic in the refrigerator.

Lightly flour a work surface and set up a pasta machine according to its instructions. Line a rimmed baking sheet with parchment paper and sprinkle flour all over. Cut the dough into 8 equal pieces and set them aside, wrapping loosely with plastic wrap. Set the pasta machine to its thickest setting. Working with 1 dough piece at a time, flatten the dough into a rectangle. Run the dough through the machine, fold in half crosswise (end to end), and run it through again. Continue, adjusting the machine to narrower settings after every 2 passes and dusting with flour as needed to keep from sticking, until the pasta sheet is about 18 inches long. Place the pasta sheet on the prepared baking sheet. Repeat with the remaining dough pieces.

Cut the rectangular pasta pieces into ¼-inch strands for fettuccine, or use the machine setting to cut strands to desired widths. Return the strands back to the prepared baking sheet. Dust the pasta with more flour to keep from sticking and cover loosely with plastic. Repeat with the remaining pasta pieces.

To use the pasta, cook it in salted boiling water, stirring occasionally, until al dente, about 2 minutes. Drain the pasta and use in your favorite pasta dish.

Ranch Cacio e Pepe

The past few years have been for cacio e pepe what the '90s were for sun-dried tomatoes. It's everywhere in restaurants and on all areas of the menu—taking on forms from pizza to ice cream. Adding ranch to pasta might seem like a sacrilegious move on the Italian staple, but it brings onions, herbs, and adds to the dish's already silky texture for a risk that you won't regret taking. This is one of the rare recipes where I'd advise you to use store-bought ranch rather than any of the homemade versions—it's less likely to break when you toss it with hot pasta. Long, thin pasta shapes are the traditional way to go, so if you're feeling bold, use the Homemade Ranch Pasta in this dish.

ingredients

1 pound dried bucatini or Homemade Ranch Pasta (page 162)
¼ cup extra-virgin olive oil
1½ tablespoons whole black peppercorns
¾ cup store-bought ranch dressing
1 cup freshly grated Parmigiano-Reggiano cheese, plus more for sprinkling
⅓ cup freshly grated Pecorino-Romano cheese, plus more for sprinkling
Kosher salt
Freshly ground black pepper

directions

In a large pot of salted boiling water over medium-high heat, cook the pasta according to the package instructions until al dente, stirring occasionally with tongs to untangle the strands. Reserve ¼ cup of the pasta water.

While the pasta cooks, in a large skillet or saucepan, heat the oil over medium heat. Add the peppercorns and toast until fragrant. Turn off the heat and return to medium heat when the pasta is al dente. Using tongs, transfer the pasta from the pot directly to the skillet with the peppercorns and oil. Stir briefly to combine and remove the skillet from the heat. Add the ranch and both cheeses, tossing the pasta constantly until a smooth sauce forms and becomes fully incorporated with the pasta. If the pasta seems dry, add the reserved pasta water until you achieve sufficient sauciness. Season with salt to taste.

To serve, transfer the pasta to bowls. Top with a few cranks of pepper and sprinkle some more Parmigiano-Reggiano and Pecorino-Romano on top.

Rice Noodles

with Coconut Cream & Shiso Ranch

This dish is loosely inspired in part by the Korean dish *kongguksu*, a cold noodle dish served in a chilled soy milk broth, often in the summer. Things take a turn toward the nontraditional once it gets ranched up with Coconut Cream & Shiso Ranch, but that tang balances out the nutty, slightly sweet broth for a surprisingly refreshing endgame.

ingredients

½ cup Coconut Cream & Shiso Ranch (page 31)

3 tablespoons soy milk

Juice from 2 limes

2 teaspoons grated ginger

2 teaspoons brown sugar

3 teaspoons fish sauce (optional)

11 ounces fresh rice noodles, such as Nona Lim

2 cups watercress, tough stems removed

8 ounces store-bought braised tofu, cut into ½-inch slices

½ cup fresh mint leaves

½ cup fresh cilantro leaves with tender stems

½ English cucumber, peeled and thinly sliced into half-moons

3 scallions, thinly sliced, soaked in ice water

2 medium radishes, thinly sliced

2 tablespoons toasted sesame seeds

Chile paste, such as Sambal Oelek, or chile oil for serving

directions

In a large bowl, whisk together the ranch, soy milk, lime juice, ginger, brown sugar, and fish sauce (if using). Set aside.

In a large saucepan, bring salted water to a boil and cook the rice noodles according to the package instructions. Drain and rinse under cold water. Set aside.

Toss the noodles with the ranch and soy mixture, watercress, and tofu. Divide among 2 bowls and top with the mint, cilantro, cucumber, scallions, radishes, and sesame seeds. When ready to serve, top with the chile paste or chile oil for added heat.

Lemongrass Ranch Curry with Shrimp

No matter your devotion to trying every curry out there, this is likely one you haven't seen before. Ranch makes two appearances in this dish: as a coconut cream base for simmering the dish and at the end as final seasoning. If you have leftover coconut cream from making the ranch, stir it into your rice as you reheat it for a slightly sweet twist.

ingredients

1 tablespoon vegetable oil

1 small shallot, finely chopped

3 garlic cloves, very finely minced

2 lemongrass stalks, bulb and pale green parts finely chopped

1 tablespoon grated ginger

1 jalapeño, stemmed, seeded, and finely chopped, plus more slices for garnish

1 cup Coconut Cream & Shiso Ranch (page 31)

¼ cup green curry paste

1 cup chicken stock

2 teaspoons Homemade Ranch Seasoning (page 38) or store-bought ranch seasoning, plus more to taste

Juice from ½ lime

Kosher salt

Freshly ground black pepper

1 pound large shrimp, peeled and deveined

4 cups cooked rice, for serving

Fresh cilantro leaves, for garnish

directions

In a medium saucepan, heat the oil over medium heat. Add the shallot, garlic, lemongrass, ginger, and jalapeño. Cook, stirring often, until the shallot becomes translucent, about 4 minutes. Add the ranch, curry paste, and chicken stock. Reduce the heat and simmer the curry, stirring occasionally, until it thickens slightly, about 20 minutes. Season with the ranch seasoning, lime juice, salt, and pepper. Add the shrimp to the curry and simmer until cooked through, about 3 minutes.

Divide the rice among 4 plates and top with the shrimp and curry. Garnish with the cilantro and jalapeño slices.

Ranch-Marinated Lamb Skewers

MAKES ABOUT 12 SKEWERS

There's that famous *Mean Girls* quote about math being the same in every language, and the same can be said for kebabs. There's some variation of meat-on-stick in many cultures around the world, all slightly different but all reliably satisfying. Ranch pulls double duty here in both the marinade and the dip, making for tender bite-size pieces that aren't sheepish on flavor.

ingredients

2 cups sour cream

2 cups plain yogurt

1 lemon, halved, plus 1 teaspoon fresh lemon juice plus more to taste

2 garlic cloves, minced

2 teaspoons onion powder

1 teaspoon mustard powder

½ teaspoon sumac (optional)

Kosher salt

2 tablespoons finely chopped fresh dill, plus more for garnish

2 tablespoons finely chopped fresh parsley, plus more for garnish

2 tablespoons finely chopped fresh mint, plus more for garnish

2 tablespoons red wine vinegar

Freshly ground black pepper

¼ cup buttermilk

2 pounds boneless lamb shoulder, trimmed, cut into 1-inch pieces

Vegetable oil, for greasing the grill

3 tablespoons honey

2 Calabrian chiles, thinly sliced

Special equipment: 12 wooden skewers, soaked in water for about 1 hour

directions

In a large bowl, combine the sour cream, yogurt, lemon juice, garlic, onion powder, mustard powder, sumac (if using), 1 tablespoon salt, dill, parsley, mint, and vinegar. Season with pepper and whisk in the buttermilk. Season with more lemon juice, salt, and pepper to taste. Transfer 1½ cups of the ranch marinade to a small bowl. Keep covered and refrigerate until ready to serve.

In a large resealable bag, combine the lamb and the remaining marinade, turning to evenly coat the lamb all over. Refrigerate overnight.

Preheat a gas or charcoal grill to medium-high heat and lightly grease the grates with oil. Remove the lamb from the marinade, wiping off any excess. Thread the lamb pieces onto the skewers, and season the skewers with salt and pepper. Grill the lamb, turning occasionally, until charred in some spots, about 7 minutes for medium doneness. Meanwhile, grill the lemon halves, cut sides down, until beautifully darkened, about 4 minutes.

Transfer the lamb skewers and lemon halves to a serving platter. Drizzle the honey over the skewers, and top with the chile slices and more dill, parsley, and mint. Squeeze the grilled lemon halves over the skewers and serve with the reserved ranch yogurt.

Steak with Watercress and Ranch Horseradish

MAKES 4 SERVINGS

You're used to seeing horseradish with prime rib, but it works just as well here to cut through the rib eye's meatiness and act as counterpoint to ranch's cooling power. Think of it like sriracha mayo, but with a different kind of heat and a better kind of mayo. Multiple butter events take this steak from just fine to prime status, as you'll baste the steak with ranch butter and dot it with more butter right before serving.

ingredients

2 (14-ounce) bone-in rib eye steaks, patted dry
Kosher salt
Freshly ground black pepper
¼ cup finely grated fresh horseradish
¼ cup Classic Ranch (page 28) or store-bought ranch dressing
2 tablespoons vegetable oil
3 garlic cloves, smashed
3 fresh rosemary sprigs
6 tablespoons (¾-stick) Ranch Compound Butter (page 39), softened
2 tablespoons extra-virgin olive oil
1 tablespoon fresh lemon juice
1 bunch watercress (about 6 ounces), tough stems removed
¼ cup fresh parsley leaves with tender stems
Flaky sea salt, for serving
Lemon wedges, for serving

directions

Liberally season the steaks with the salt and pepper. Let the steaks come to room temperature before cooking, about 45 minutes. Meanwhile, in a small bowl combine the horseradish and the ranch. Season with salt and a generous amount of pepper.

In a large cast-iron skillet, heat the vegetable oil over medium-high heat until the oil is shimmering and begins to smoke. Carefully add the steaks, garlic, and rosemary sprigs to the skillet (if the steaks seem overcrowded, cook in batches). Sear the steaks until a crust begins to develop, about 4 minutes. Flip them and continue to cook for about 4 minutes. Add 3 tablespoons ranch butter to the skillet. Tilt the skillet to pool the butter to one side of the pan and baste the steaks with the ranch butter. Cook the steaks until browned and seared, about 7 minutes total for the second side. For medium-rare, an instant-read thermometer should read 135°F when inserted into the thickest part of the steak. Transfer the steaks to a cutting board and let rest for 15 minutes.

Meanwhile, in a medium bowl combine the olive oil, lemon juice, watercress, and parsley. Season with salt and pepper, and toss to combine.

Dot the steaks with the remaining 3 tablespoons ranch butter. Carve them and sprinkle flaky sea salt all over. Serve the slices of steak with the watercress salad, ranch horseradish, and lemon wedges.

All That Glitters:
Jewel-Encrusted Ranch Bottle

If anything were to sum up ranch's tendencies to show up in both the highest and lowest of places, it would be the 75-carat bottle decked out in sapphires, diamonds, and gold that Hidden Valley made to celebrate National Ranch Day in 2018.

They called it a "one-of-a-kind" bottle, which is a lie, because while one random person will win their own as the result of a social media contest, another is being sent to the United Kingdom as a wedding gift for Prince Harry and Meghan Markle. It's at once a metaphor for the union of a celebrity and British royalty, and a reminder that no wedding registry will ever be good enough in comparison.

The bottle is valued at $35,000, which is 6,000 times more than standard-grade ones (i.e. no jewels, 0 karats, plastic) you'd find at the grocery store. But those don't come with a crown as a bottle top, so you decide which is a better use of your money.

Index

Note: Page numbers in *italics* refer to photographs

About the Author

After graduating from Yale with a degree in neuroscience and psychology, Abby Reisner moved to New York to attend the culinary arts program at the International Culinary Center. She's a food writer, editor, cook, and digital strategist living in Brooklyn, and is currently the content director at TastingTable.com. Much like the ranch craze, she's a product of the '90s.

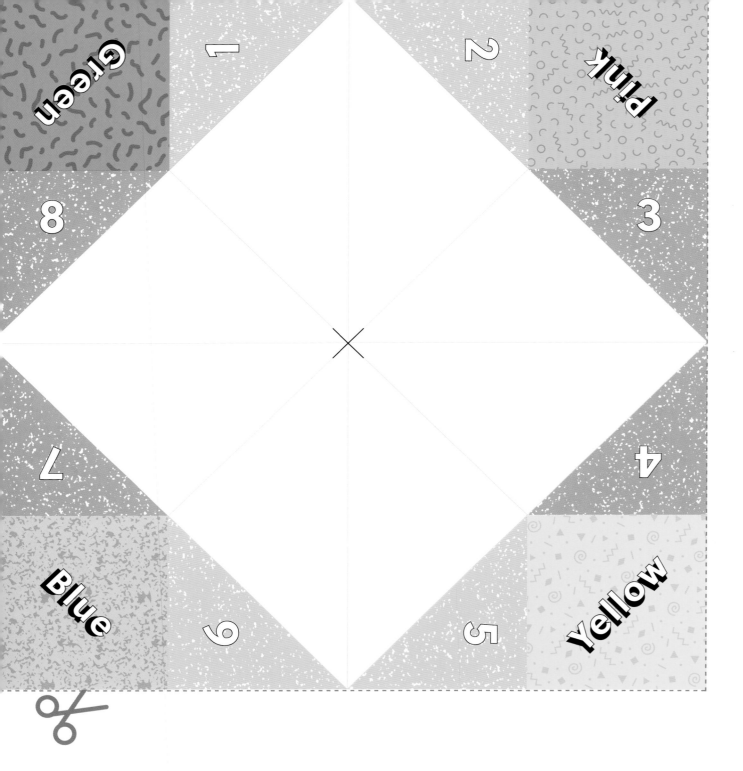

Green

1

2

Pink

8

3

7

4

Blue

6

5

Yellow

The Fortune Teller

Make your own version of this '90s relic. Cut out the fortune teller on the opposite page and write in your own fortunes—one in each white triangle for a total of eight fortunes. Fold your fortune teller and you're ready to play!

1.

2.

3.

4.

5.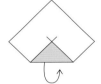

6.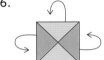

7.

8.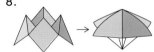

How to play:

1. While holding the fortune teller with your thumbs and index fingers, ask a friend to pick a color on one of the four outer flaps. Spell out the color while opening the fortune teller horizontally and vertically with your fingers, once for each letter.

2. When you're done spelling out the color, the inner flap will reveal four numbers. Have your friend choose one of the numbers, then count it out the same way you spelled out the color, by opening the fortune teller horizontally or vertically once for each number.

3. Once you're done counting out the number the inner flap will reveal four numbers. Ask your friend to pick one of the numbers again, then lift up the flap and read the fortune underneath that number.

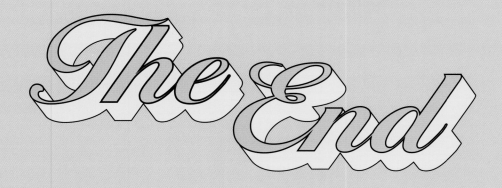

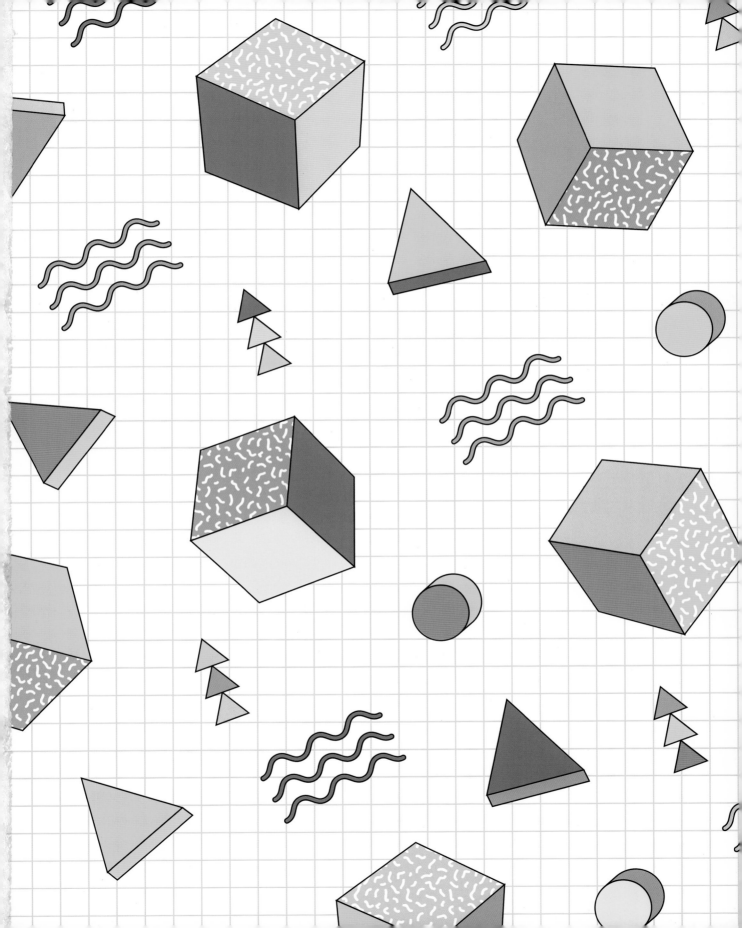

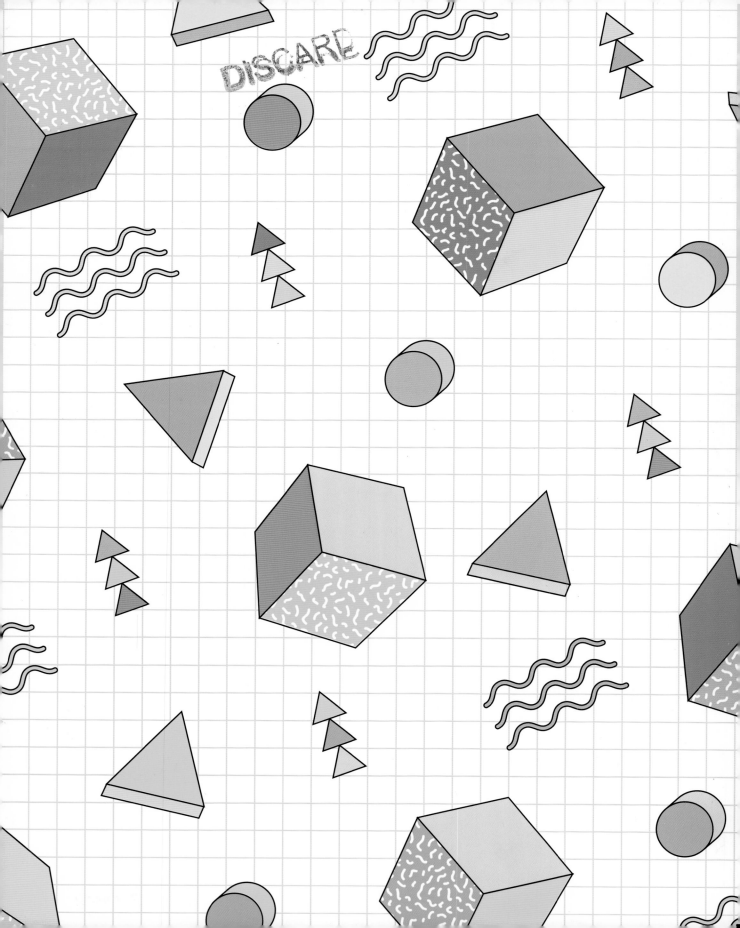